POLITICS AND
PLANNERS

Gary W. Wynia

POLITICS AND PLANNERS / Economic
Development Policy in
Central America

THE UNIVERSITY OF WISCONSIN PRESS

Published 1972
The University of Wisconsin Press
Box 1379, Madison, Wisconsin 53701

The University of Wisconsin Press, Ltd.
70 Great Russell Street, London

For LC CIP information see the colophon page

ISBN 0–299–06210–4

For Annie and Art

CONTENTS

TABLES

FIGURES

MAP

ACKNOWLEDGMENTS

To STUDY PUBLIC POLICY-MAKING one must have the co-operation of public officials. It was my good fortune to have enjoyed such cooperation throughout Central America. Many of those who offered their time, insights, and files have devoted their lives to observing and affecting Central American development; I hope that I have faithfully reported some of the lessons they have learned.

Several sources of information have been tapped for this study. During 1968 and 1969 I examined documents and interviewed national planners and other public officials in the Central American governments and in several regional and international agencies. At the end of the book the reader will find a Note on Sources which explains my use of documentary and interview data. The field work and initial writing of the study were supported by fellowships from the University of Wisconsin and The Brookings Institution in Washington, D.C.

Carl Akins, Abraham Lowenthal, M. Crawford Young, and James Cochrane have read parts of the manuscript and offered numerous suggestions for its improvement, and Philippe Schmitter stimulated a much needed clarification of its final focus and design. Two people have shared in this project since its beginning and merit special recognition. Charles W. Anderson tirelessly guided me through the labyrinths of development policy-making and Latin American politics with the boundless energy and unceasing curiosity that have enriched all of those who have worked with him. My wife Ann, who accompanied me along the roads and trails of Central America, assisted in the recording of numerous materials. For never tiring of development plans, highways, and houses she has earned my admiration and gratitude.

Minneapolis, Minnesota   GARY W. WYNIA
March, 1972

POLITICS AND
PLANNERS

1

Introduction

THIS IS A STUDY OF INNOVATIONS and their consequences on the policy-making processes of five Central American nations. The principal innovators were the economists and engineers, or *técnicos*, who, supported largely by international agencies, sought to reshape national policy-making processes, expand development programs, and reform antiquated bureaucracies. Their principal adversaries were the presidents and the bureaucrats whose policies and agencies they tried to change.

From the perspective of the *técnicos* who staffed Central America's national planning agencies, the decade of the 1960s ended with bitter disappointments. Buoyed by an optimism induced by their United Nations training programs and the promises of moral and financial support under the Alliance for Progress, they enthusiastically immersed themselves in the designing of ambitious development programs as the decade began. Initially ignored, or at least tolerated, by their own governments, the five national planning agencies quickly produced Five Year Plans for the 1965–69 period and eagerly set about their implementation. Suddenly, however, their paths were strewn with unanticipated obstacles as presidents failed to provide financial support for the ambitious programs and bureaucrats hesitated and balked at their implementation. As the decade

3

ended the programs remained largely unfulfilled and the *técnicos* found themselves still without much influence in national policy-making processes. To many it appeared that they had established decorative rather than indicative planning in Central America.

From the Central American presidents' perspective, on the other hand, the decade seemed merely a continuation of their efforts to harmonize demands for new development policies with the requirements of their traditional political structures and the vicissitudes of their unstable export economies. To the presidents, success appeared to be measured not in the fulfillment of specific development program objectives but in their own survival in power, and the former, they recognized, was not necessarily a means to the latter. On the contrary, they frequently acted as if the longevity of their tenure depended on their ability to deter their planners' efforts to implement development programs.

For the student of development policy-making the Central American experience raises some important questions about the process of policy innovation in developing countries. First, why did the planners fail to reach their public investment objectives? How did specific economic, political, technical, and bureaucratic conditions contribute to their shortcomings? Second, why did an adversary rather than a more cooperative relationship develop between planners and presidents? Should not we have expected a rather bumpy, but accommodating mutual adjustment between planners and presidents? And, finally, despite the general pattern of quantitative shortcomings and mutual hostility, were there any differences in the performances of the five Central American countries? Did not the fact that one was ruled by a personalistic authoritarian ruler and another by an open, competitive political process have some impact on the implementation of development programs? Or put another way, what were the contrasting consequences of authoritarian and democratic rule on program success or failure? To answer these questions we must first begin by placing Central America within its proper perspective.

THE LATIN AMERICAN CONTEXT

Historically and culturally the Central American states are part of Latin America. As such, one might expect that their policy-making processes would reflect patterns similar to the other, though generally larger, Latin American states. Bearing this in mind, we can begin our examination of Central American policy-making within its Latin American context.

It is of course impossible to identify "the" Latin American environment or "the" Latin American policy-making structure in any detail, for there is much variation among the political systems of the area. Nevertheless, we can, thanks to the path-finding work of a few scholars, identify some characteristics that appear to prevail, with slight variations and a few exceptions, throughout Latin America.[1] By synthesizing these observations we can identify the region's principal policy-making patterns. From them we can try to create hypotheses about the probable behavior of planners within Latin America.

Seven characteristics appear to form what might be termed the policy-making structure of the Latin American countries. These are:

1. Personalistic, and often charismatic, leadership juxtaposed with a lack of institutional, especially constitutional, legitimacy;
2. Expanding political participation, yet political underrepresentation of the urban and rural masses;
3. Administrative structures dominated by extensive patronage, intricate formal rules, and widespread informal disregard for formal rules;

1. The list is drawn from the following works: Charles W. Anderson, *Politics and Economic Change in Latin America* (Princeton: D. Van Nostrand, 1967); John Friedmann, *The Social Context of National Planning Decisions: A Comparative Approach* (Bloomington, Ind.: CAG Occasional Paper, 1964); Albert O. Hirschman, *Journeys Toward Progress* (New York: Anchor Books, 1965); and Nathaniel Leff, *Economic Policy-Making and Development in Brazil 1947–1964* (New York: John Wiley and Sons, 1968).

4. Obscured and obstructed communications within the public sector and between the public and private sectors produced by weak information as well as by distrust and personal rivalries;

5. A heavy reliance on the private sector for managing but not financing economic growth;

6. Slow economic growth and modernization because of numerous structural and institutional rigidities;

7. Economic dependence on foreign markets and, as a consequence, vulnerability to external economic and financial conditions.

When combined, these characteristics form an "ideal type" that looks as follows: we find personalistic leaders who direct patronage-ridden bureaucracies, enjoy weak communications with other power contenders, and receive inadequate information from government agencies and the private sector, yet must struggle to raise large revenues to support programs to expand their vulnerable and sluggish economies.

How is policy made under such conditions? Charles Anderson and Albert Hirschman have identified two contrasting responses by Latin American policy-makers operating in this environment. At one extreme on the continuum are the insecure, ill-informed policy-makers who proceed in a very tentative or cautious manner. Each step or policy change is a small one because of both the policy-maker's inability to predict its impact and his fear of adverse consequences. His thinking is guided by a "small risk, small loss" sense of caution. Only after assuring the maintenance of his political position will he continue to expand his policy initiatives. At the other extreme on the continuum we find the policy-maker grasping at totally unrealistic policy schemes. His desire to solve complex problems far outruns his understanding of them and he becomes extremely vulnerable to pseudo-insights and pseudo-solutions. Rather than avoiding or cautiously tinkering with a policy problem, he plunges into it guided by a belief that personal energy or elaborate conceptualization of the solution will compensate for his ignorance. Neither Anderson nor Hirschman predicts which of these paths the policy-makers will travel; instead, they leave us to examine policy choices case by case in search of further explanation.[2] This we will do in the analysis of the Central American experience.

The next logical question concerns the fate of the planners and their policy innovations. How will development planners perform when confronted by the Latin American policy-making styles just described? Unfortunately, there is no satisfactory answer, for a variety of contrasting hypotheses can be produced by our characterization of Latin American policy-making. Such hypotheses are easily produced because of the potential variation in the impact of the planners on the policy-making structure or, conversely, of the policy-making structure on the planners. In essence, the planners seek to alter policy-making processes by creating new institutions, improving administration of existing institutions, acquiring more policy information, and guiding the economy to greater productivity. At the same time, they are part of a multi-variate process in which each of their actions will be hindered or aided by traditional policy-making structures. Consequently, one can envision Latin American planners manifesting a variety of behavior patterns. They might, for example, conform to the style of the cautious policy-maker because they too lack information and frequently distrust other executive agencies. Their caution might lead to a scaling down of their ambitious development programs and their focusing instead on policy bottlenecks, short-range revenue and investment programs, and the coordination of only a few agencies and policies. Only after gradually gaining more information and control would they venture beyond these narrow pursuits. It is equally plausible that the planners might blend with the policy-maker who immerses himself in utopian schemes. There is in fact a natural harmony between the ill-informed yet highly motivated policy-maker and the ambitious and overeager planner who becomes obsessed with the pseudo-precision and comprehensiveness of his paper plans.

This attempt at synthesizing the principal characteristics of

2. Anderson, *Politics*, Chaps. 3–5; Hirschman, *Journeys*, Chap. 4.

Latin American policy-making processes serves to initiate specu-
lation about the impact of planners in Latin America, but it
falls far short of predicting the nature of that impact. It has
drawn our attention to some of the characteristics of the policy-
making structures that planners may encounter. Their responses
to each, however, may vary along a continuum between rather
widely dispersed extremes. Logical deduction, then, has taken us
only a short distance; to continue our search we must turn to
empirical inquiry by focusing on the experience of the Central
American countries. Let us begin with an examination of their
political processes and then proceed to the analysis of their
development policy innovations during the United Nations Development Decade of the 1960s.

CENTRAL AMERICA IN PERSPECTIVE

The common image of Central America is a narrow strip of
land connecting North and South America, noted primarily for
its banana crops and its dormant people whose energies have
been repressed by petty dictators. In fact, this strip of land includes 170,000 square miles, a little more than the state of California. It does produce bananas, but in the 1960s coffee accounted for 43 percent of export earnings, cotton 22 percent,
and bananas only 14 percent.[3] Political instability and numerous
forms of dictatorial rule have appeared in the region since its
independence from Spain was achieved in 1821, yet the region
has also witnessed some interesting experiments in democratic
rule, military governments, and leftist revolutionary regimes.

While there are historical and cultural justifications for cate-
gorizing Central America as a region, there is much that serves
to make these five countries very distinct. Despite Spanish rule
over the region by a Captaincy General in Guatemala until 1821,
local isolation resulting from harsh mountainous terrain and the
consequent creation of powerful local administrative centers

3. ECLA, *Economic Survey of Latin America—1965* (New York,
1967), p. 169.

stimulated a sense of autonomy among the small, but numerous population centers of the region. The towns of Guatemala, Quetzaltenango, Comayagua, San Salvador, Leon, Granada, and Cartago became the homes of the little armies that followed local leaders through the constant and bloody struggles that characterized the first half of the nineteenth century. These struggles established the patterns of political development in nineteenth-century Central America and the territorial claims of these administrative centers form the basis for the creation of nation-states during the post-independence period. Beginning its independence with very meager resources and fewer than 1 million inhabitants, the region reached the end of the nineteenth century exhausted and impoverished. The towns remained the dominant forces in their countries, border demarcations continued unresolved, and little effort was made to integrate the remaining Indian and rural populations into unified nations.

The struggles did not cease, but their frequency diminished by the early twentieth century. Exhaustion, consolidation of forces by some local leaders, and actual and threatened intervention by the United States brought greater stability to the region. Battles between states were much fewer and strong-arm rulers managed to impose political order for extended periods, particularly after 1925. The economic development of the region was left to local coffee producers after 1850 and foreign banana interests after 1870. Some infrastructure growth followed these developments, but it concentrated around the needs of the foreign enterprises and the local export economy. By 1960 the Central American nations shared many similiarities. At the same time, there were many important, though often subtle differences among the five countries. A brief examination of their economic and political structures reveals some of these similiarities and differences.

Central America is a small part of Latin America. Its 11 million inhabitants in 1960 were only 5 percent of the Latin American total. Yet, variations within the region are significant once its small scale is recognized. In physical size the extremes range from tiny El Salvador's 8,260 square miles (about the size of Massachusetts) to Nicaragua's 57,145 square miles (about the size of Illinois) and in population from Costa Rica's 1.2 million in 1960 to Guatemala's 4 million.[4]

Even more than in most of Latin America, the Central American economies are dominated by agriculture. While a majority of the rural labor force is occupied in subsistence farming, the moving forces of the region's economy are the commercial banana, coffee, and cotton producers who are entirely oriented toward foreign markets. Largely due to their efforts, the gross domestic product of the combined Central American economies grew at an average annual rate of 4.2 percent between 1948 and 1960, only slightly below the Latin American average of 4.4 percent during that period.[5] Within Central America the extremes ranged from 3.3 percent in Guatemala to 6.0 percent in Nicaragua. Yet, despite these relatively favorable growth rates, Central America's per capita incomes continued far behind the Latin American average during the period (see Table 1).

TABLE 1
Per Capita Income, 1961

Costa Rica	$362.00
El Salvador	$268.00
Guatemala	$258.00
Honduras	$252.00
Nicaragua	$288.00
Central American Average	*$285.00*
Latin American Average	*$421.00*

Source: United Nations, *The Economic Development of Latin America in the Post-War Period* (New York, 1964), p. 51.

Aggregate measures of productivity and income provide only a partial view of Central American economic conditions; equally important are indices of structural rigidities. Like their fellow Latin Americans, the Central Americans have tied themselves to external markets since the late nineteenth century. Initially,

4. ECLA, *Estudio económico de América Latina—1968* (Mexico City, 1969), p. 6
5. United Nations, *The Economic Development of Latin America in the Post-War Period* (New York, 1964), p. 18.

the export-oriented development strategy generated rapid growth in the once stagnant economies of the region. As commercial agriculture replaced many unproductive *haciendas*, foreign investors supplied capital for new agricultural enterprises and transportation infrastructure, and governments reaped new revenues from export and import taxation. By the late 1950s, however, a rapid decline in export prices brought recognition of the vulnerability of the Central American economies. The impact of the export price decline is revealed clearly by the region's terms of trade in the late 1950s: using 1955 as an index year of 100, the terms of trade for the Central American countries in the aggregate declined to 76 by 1960; this decline was even greater than the Latin American average, which dropped to 87 during the same period.[6] No condition has more challenged and frustrated the planners during the 1960s than this one.

Turning to Central America's political structures, one discovers many of the traits that are observable throughout Latin America. Like the Venezuelans and the Mexicans, the Central Americans suffered under *caudillo*-led violence during the nineteenth century. Their territory was occupied by foreign armies as was that of Mexico, Cuba, Haiti, and the Dominican Republic. In the twentieth century they have had their share of strong-arm dictators, military coups, and assassinations. Nevertheless, the Central American political processes are by no means carbon copies of each other nor of the rest of Latin America. The range of Central American political phenomena can be seen through a comparison of the five systems along three dimensions: government structure, political competition, and militarism.

Since World War II the Central American governments have followed the trend toward the expansion of governmental responsibilities and institutions set by the larger Latin American states after the 1929 world depression. In the past two decades government agencies, budgets, and personnel have proliferated in all five countries. Costa Rican expansion has been the most gradual, yet the most complete in the region. Its small but concentrated population developed a sense of nationhood and policy

6. Ibid., p. 130.

expectations earlier than its neighbors: public education was extended to all urban residents in the 1880s, a public insurance agency and a mortgage bank were created in the 1930s, and a social security program was added in the mid-1940s. The other Central American governments joined the expansionary bandwagon in the late 1940s and early 1950s with the expansion of line agencies and the creation of central banks, development banks, and numerous autonomous agencies to manage new economic and social programs. By 1963 Costa Rica, for example, had 19,796 government employees, 11,990 of whom worked in fifty autonomous agencies. The other Central American governments, though tending toward less decentralization, possessed similar structures and personnel distributions in 1963.[7]

The selection of personnel has been dominated by patronage in all five countries. Only Costa Rica and El Salvador had managed to create merit systems by 1960, but even these two systems applied to a minority of government employees. One observer of the Honduran bureaucracy during the early 1950s concluded that:

The slogan "to the victor belongs the spoils" means, in Honduras, that personal and partisan factors dominate all phases of administration, at every level of government . . . in the Honduran spoils system, particularly in respect to the appointment of officers, a disproportionate emphasis is placed upon personal loyalty to the leader. Indeed, *personalismo* might well be defined as principle in the Honduran administrative process. The average man too frequently feels

---

7. The number of government personnel in the five countries in 1963 was as follows:

	Total Public Sector
Costa Rica	19,796
El Salvador	21,722
Guatemala	18,698
Honduras	14,060
Nicaragua	14,357

Instituto Centroamericano de Administración Pública (ICAP), *Recursos humanos: el sector público y la situación actual en Centroamérica* (San José, 1968), p. 8.

little or no responsibility for the efficient operation of government, a feeling which is in part a carry-over of colonial tradition.[8]

Similiar observations have been made in the other four countries, where the impact of patronage has varied only with the degree of political competition and the frequency of changing administrations.

Jealously guarded agency autonomy was another outstanding characteristic of Central American administration in the early 1960s. The creation of autonomous agencies was the product of administrative strategies prevailing throughout Latin America after World War II. Some argued that agency autonomy guaranteed freedom from autocratic presidential control. This view was explicitly incorporated into the Costa Rican Constitution of 1949.[9] Others argued that autonomy would permit specialization and unity of direction in each policy area. Perhaps most common, though, was the appeal of autonomy to those policy innovators who feared the capture and destruction of new programs by the ill-equipped and poorly managed line agencies. By securing new management for each new program, one could free it from such hazards; or so it was believed.

By the time the planners arrived in the early 1960s, the liabilities as well as the benefits of autonomy had become clearly apparent, particularly in such an intensely decentralized system as the Costa Rican. Economic programming required greater central direction and control, yet with autonomy there developed numerous suspicious and independent centers of administrative power that defied central coordination. When faced by the challenge of development programming, the once optimistic Costa Ricans concluded that: "functional decentralization offers a contradictory picture of the creation of a structure that, by definition, ought to make the action of the state stronger in economic policy-making; but, as it now functions it is going in

8. William S. Stokes, *Honduras: An Area Study in Government* (Madison: The University of Wisconsin Press, 1950), p. 191.

9. See, for example, Wilberg Jimenez Castro, *Las dilemas de la decentralización funcional* (San José: ESAPAC, 1965).

the opposite direction, that is, toward the weakening of the power of the state to act." [10]

It is apparent that in 1960 the planners encountered not unified, highly trained, and motivated Central American bureaucracies but ones that had undergone rapid change and expansion during the preceding decade and were floundering under the competing claims and goals of a variety of new administrative agencies. Patronage had produced individual loyalty to particular patrons within each agency and not to the regime or the president, and, most of all, not to those uninvited intruders, the development planners.

Political scientists have long recognized the importance of political competition and continue to debate its impact on public policy. [11] Measurements of political competition have focused primarily on political parties in the electoral process and have assumed regularized electoral competition and a certain degree of party stability. These assumptions, however, are not entirely valid for Central America. Guatemala and Honduras, for example, have not held elections at regularly scheduled intervals during the past two decades but have experienced military coups and irregular election schedules. In addition, party instability was high in Guatemala, and in Honduras the two presidents who served longest during the 1950–70 period were elected by constituent assemblies, not by direct popular vote.

Despite these irregularities, we can compare party competition in the five countries through brief descriptions of their party systems. Costa Rica clearly has the most stable and competitive electoral process. The average percentage vote difference between the two leading presidential candidates was only 11.8 percent in four elections between 1953 and 1966. [12] More indica-

10. ICAP, *Estudio sobre las instituciones autonomas de Costa Rica* (San José, 1967), p. 71. All translations are mine.

11. See, for example, Richard E. Dawson and James A. Robinson, "Inter-Party Competition, Economic Variables and Welfare in the American States," *Journal of Politics* 25 (1963): 265–89; and Thomas R. Dye, *Politics, Economics and the Public* (Chicago: Rand McNally & Co., 1966).

12. Institute for the Comparative Study of Political Systems, *Costa Rica Election Factbook—February 6, 1966* (Washington, 1965) and

tive of its competitiveness is the fact that none of the three leading parties has controlled the presidency for two consecutive terms since 1948. Guatemala and Honduras are also competitive systems in that no single party has dominated either government continually since 1950. Party success in both systems, however, is as much a product of military support as electoral victory. The two leading Guatemalan presidential candidates were separated by an average of only 9.9 percent of the vote in the 1958 and 1966 presidential elections. The two elections were separated, however, by a military coup in 1963 that eliminated from the 1966 election the party that had won in 1958.[13] Honduras' only two parties were separated by an average of 17.7 percent of the vote in the 1957 and the 1965 constituent assembly elections. But these data are also deceptive. The Liberal party, which won the 1957 elections, was overthrown by the military, which then joined with the opposition Nationalist party to guarantee its election in 1965.

In contrast to their neighbors, El Salvador and Nicaragua have been ruled by one-party regimes during the past two decades. El Salvador's ruling political party received an average of 59 percent more votes than its nearest competitor in four presidential elections between 1950 and 1967. In Nicaragua the average difference between the Somoza family's National Liberal party and the opposition Conservative party averaged 80 percent in the 1957, 1963, and 1967 elections.[14]

Political party competition in Central America obviously does not conform to the stereotype of small impoverished states completely under dictatorial control. Yet, with the exception of

---

John Martz, "Costa Rican Electoral Trends," *The Western Political Quarterly* 20 (December, 1967): 896–912.

13. Institute for the Comparative Study of Political Systems, *Guatemala Election Factbook—March 6, 1966* (Washington, 1966); and Kenneth F. Johnson, *The Guatemalan Presidential Election of March 6, 1966: An Analysis* (Washington: Institute for the Comparative Study of Political Systems, 1967).

14. Institute for the Comparative Study of Political Systems, *El Salvador Election Factbook—March 5, 1967* and *Nicaragua Election Factbook—February 5, 1967* (Washington, 1966).

Costa Rica, neither does it conform to most competitive models, for during the past two decades the rules and results of the electoral game have been frequently altered. In Guatemala and Honduras such alterations have given one party an opportunity to eliminate another, while in El Salvador and Nicaragua they have produced strong one-party regimes. We are concerned, however, not only with the democratic purity of these systems, but also with their effects on development policy-making. For example, was the competitive Costa Rican system more receptive to development planners and their innovations than the more authoritarian Nicaraguan system? We will examine this question in the chapters that follow.

In his analysis of Latin American militaries, Edwin Lieuwen identified those of Central America as among the more backward, personalistic, and least institutionalized in the hemisphere.[15] There is no single index that measures the degree of military involvement in Central American politics. The number of coups is an artificial indicator, for militaries have controlled policy-making without coups d' etat. Conversely, they have carried out numerous coups only to return power immediately to civilian control. Whatever the indicator, Costa Rica stands out once again as the exception to the regional pattern. Its small, undisciplined army was humiliated by the popular civilian forces of José Figueres during the Revolution of 1948. Disgust with the military that had fought against civilians was so strong that the new constitutional government disbanded the army and replaced it with a 1,200-man national police force. Unique among Central Americans, Costa Rican policy-makers are free of the anxieties created by an activist military.

The other four countries share more similarities with each other than with Costa Rica, for each has an activist military, although their forms of activism have differed. The El Salvadorian military, more than any of the others, has ruled directly since 1948. It has done so, however, through its leadership of a widely organized mass-based political party. In Nicaragua the military

15. Edwin Lieuwen, "The Latin American Military," in United States Senate, Committee on Foreign Relations, *Survey of the Alliance for Progress* (April 29, 1969), p. 99.

is quite conspicuous but its role is a very special one. It has not intervened in government through periodic coups as have the Guatemalan and Honduran militaries, nor ruled directly as has the Salvadorian military. Rather, it has been an essential mainstay of the Somoza regime since 1936. The Somozas have understood the necessity of presidential monopolization of a force that loyally and efficiently imposes public order. As head of the National Guard left by American Marines in 1935, the elder Somoza learned that lesson and passed it on to his youngest son, who, after being trained at West Point, directed the National Guard until his election to the presidency in 1967. Through the use of lower class recruitment, financial favors, and military honors as well as threats of punishment, the Somozas have employed their small but efficient 5,400-man National Guard as an effective and loyal instrument of their regime.

The Honduran and Guatemalan militaries have deposed presidents periodically over the past few decades. For example, on October 21, 1955, a group of young Honduran officers overthrew President Julio Lozano, who two weeks earlier had been elected in fraudulent elections after systematically exiling his Liberal party opposition. In September 1957 the same young officers permitted the Liberal party to capture the presidency and a majority of legislative seats in the most honest election in Honduran history. However, six years later the military, resenting the Liberals' creation of a Civil Guard and threats to rescind the military's semi-autonomous constitutional status, overthrew the Liberal government. Seeking to perpetuate their rule, yet responsive to foreign demands for civilian rule, the military leaders formed a coalition with the Nationalist party and in 1965 guaranteed the election of Colonel López Arellano, the leader of the 1963 coup.

Guatemala has long been ruled by military men, e.g., Ubico, Arbenz, Castillo Armas, Ydígoras, and Peralta, but only in recent years has the military establishment tended toward regnancy. Guatemala's 9,000-man military is the largest in Central America. Since 1944 the military has grown in strength, increased in incorporation, and strengthened its professionalization. But this institutional evolution has not led to greater civilian control over the military, for, as internal political conflict has increased in the post-1944 period, so have the political and administrative functions of the military. Direct military involvement in policymaking blossomed in 1962 as officers assumed most of the cabinet posts in the rapidly deteriorating Ydígoras regime. They took direct control in March 1963, but returned the government to civilians in 1966.[16]

This brief review of government structure, political competition, and military intervention has drawn attention to some of the similarities and differences among the Central American political systems. Before concluding this introduction, a brief but more detailed description of forms of political combat in each system will be useful for a later comparison of the impact of political system differences on development programs.

Costa Rica

Costa Ricans see their country as unique within Central America because of its successful constitutional system. They have come to view elections, legislatures, and peaceful successions of presidents as peculiarly Costa Rican phenomena.[17] Since their Revolution of 1948 they have enjoyed impressive political stability. Even the Costa Rican revolution was a rather mild affair. In essence, it was a manifestation of increased, but limited demands on government rather than a struggle radically to change society. The political values guiding the revolution fit well into the Costa Rican political tradition, for the absence of a rigidly stratified social structure or an effective political tyranny

16. In his recent study of the Guatemalan military Richard N. Adams concluded: "While it has broadened its position in the society at large, it has consistently consolidated its mechanisms and bases of control. It is in a position to take over the government whenever conditions indicate that it should, and it is capable of ruling for an indefinite period." See "The Development of the Guatemalan Military," *Studies in Comparative International Development* 4 (1968–69): 107.

17. Depending on the level of sophistication of the bearer of these beliefs, the conventional explanations for Costa Rican uniqueness range from the absence of "contamination" by the Indian or the Negro to the impact of a system of universal education that has taught Costa Ricans their civic virtues.

gave little cause for the radicalization of the uprising of 1948.

By the early 1950s a three-party system had emerged dominated by the widely organized National Liberation party (PLN). Led by the energetic José Figueres since 1948, the PLN is the most professional of the three parties. Except for Figueres' landslide victory in 1953, support for the party has fluctuated between 48.8 percent and 53.6 percent in presidential elections.[18] The two other parties, the National Union party (PUN) and the Republican party (PR) represent the conservative opposition to the PLN and combined behind one candidate to win the presidency in 1966. Prior to that election, the presidency had been held twice by the PLN and twice by the PUN since 1949.

The distribution of legislative representation since 1948 has enhanced legislative influence over the Costa Rican president. The election of president and deputies is held every four years.[19] After the 1953 election the PLN president enjoyed his party's majority of 30 out of 45 deputies. The PUN president elected in 1958 had only 10 of 45 deputies and had to seek support from 15 minor party deputies. The PLN president elected in 1962 relied on a slight majority of 29 out of 57 deputies, but the conservative coalition president elected in 1966 was frequently opposed by a slight PLN majority of 29 out of 57 deputies.[20] Thus, more than any of his Central American counterparts, the Costa Rican president and his political party have been forced to cope with active electoral and legislative opposition.

Nicaragua

Nicaragua stands in contrast to Costa Rica. While sharing an Hispanic heritage, these two countries have followed different patterns of development and are governed by dissimilar political

18. Martz, "Costa Rican Electoral Trends," pp. 896–97.

19. Costa Rica has a unicameral legislature, as do all of the Central American countries except Nicaragua where it is bicameral. The Costa Rican legislature has 57 members (raised from 45 in 1961) who are elected through a system of proportional representation. A completely new membership is elected every four years, for deputies are prohibited from serving two consecutive terms.

20. Institute for the Comparative Study of Political Institutions, *Costa Rican Election Factbook*, pp. 27–32.

processes. Politics in Nicaragua are not unique in the same sense as in Costa Rica, for in place of a gradual reduction of violence and its replacement by constitutional order, the violent struggles of the Nicaraguans have been ended only by the imposition of strong-arm rule.

Anastasio Somoza, who ruled directly or indirectly from the departure of American Marines in the early 1930s until his assassination in 1956, learned many lessons from the American occupation of his country. He discovered that political order, however imposed, would bring him foreign benefactors. Avoiding the fiscal chaos of the period preceding American intervention, he managed his government efficiently and, as a consequence, became a recipient of foreign confidence and financial credit. His two sons, Luis and Anastasio Jr., benefitted from his teaching. The private economic empire built by their father has thrived on their conservative fiscal and monetary policies, and their maintenance of political stability has brought Nicaragua strong foreign support.

Unlike the authoritarian regimes of the nineteenth century, the Somozas have not been content with plunder and stagnation. They have tied themselves to Nicaragua's economic growth and have made its development synonomous with that of their own economic empire. Their investments are not in unproductive *latifundias* but in the national airline, a cement factory, a steel mill, rice and cotton plantations, sugar refineries, and cotton gins. The young Somozas have learned that there are large profits in the development business, especially for those who can control both political and economic competition. Yet the Somozas are not alone in these economic pursuits, for a favored minority of Nicaraguan agricultural entrepreneurs have attached themselves to this development enterprise. As long as the ambitions of this favored group have led to furthering the Somoza development effort rather than to competing with it, they have been welcome. Without an appreciation of these dual entrepreneurial and political roles of Nicaraguan presidents, their use of development opportunities cannot be understood.

The political style of the Somoza regime has become more

sophisticated in recent years. Although the eldest son, Luis, became president after his father's death in 1956, he permitted a long-time Somoza administrator to succeed him in 1963. The youngest son, Anastasio Somoza Debayle, was elected in 1967 and ruled as the last of the three Somozas since the death of Luis in late 1967. The Somozas campaign extensively during elections, they tolerate a weak opposition press, they enforce their father's grant of minority representation to opposition parties on all government commissions and boards, and they guarantee one-third of the legislative seats to opposition parties.

Despite the Somozas' gestures toward an open political process, Nicaraguan political life is in fact completely dominated by the presidency. Not only has their National Liberal party controlled over two-thirds of the national legislature since 1936, but they have persistently suppressed any opposition efforts to organize vocal protests. As the Nicaraguans publicly admit, "for the Nicaraguan people the Executive Power, exercised by the president, represents the entire government. Because precise definitions of the functional limits of each branch do not exist, there is a tendency for the president to extend his arena of operation, overlooking questions of jurisdiction."[21]

The pattern of presidential power that emerges in contemporary Nicaragua is characterized by two factors: presidential control over all major decisions and personalistic dominance iʳ his dealing with subordinates. No major allocations of pu' ⸱ resources are made by public officials without presiden*ᵗ' ap- proval, whether or not the law grants them authori*ᵗʸ a re- sult, the Somozas have made the command ⸝ ⸝tail one of their strongest personal attributes. They ⸻ ⸺ ₂nformation in order to anticipate reactions by key eco⸻₂mic and adminis- ᵗrative actors involved in the implementation of programs and ₂ collect such information they stress personal contact with, ₁d often intimidation of, subordinates. For the Somozas both ⸱ressive opposition and presidential isolation are intolerable.

ı. ESAPAC, *Diagnostico y macroanálisis administrativo del sector* ⸍*ico de la República de Nicaragua* (San José, 1964), p. 1.

Honduras

Honduras differs from both Costa Rica and Nicaragua. During the past fifty years the Hondurans have experienced dictatorial rule, fraudulent elections, military coups, an honest election, traditionalism, and reformism. Dictatorial rule was the product of the personalistic dominance of Tiburcio Cariás between 1933 and 1948; a relatively honest election in 1957 led to the abortive reformism of Dr. Villeda Morales; and a fraudulent election was used by the military to legitimate its rule in 1965. Honduras has not been dominated by consolidated presidential power like Nicaragua nor has it enjoyed regularized electoral competition like Costa Rica; instead, it has been ruled by any coalition of forces that could impose some form of political order on the country's regional centers of economic and political power.

Since the late nineteenth century Honduras has sustained a form of the two-party system. These are not two parties that consistently represent specific class interests nor have they competed openly in elections on more than a few occasions. Rather, they are loosely organized groupings scattered throughout the country, which, through their adherence to political party symbols rather than specific policies, have developed strong patterns of identification among the Honduran masses. While the Liberal party is identified as more reformist than the Nationalist party, the support of both parties comes from all social classes.

Political cleavages resulting from identification with the two parties are found in most Honduran towns and villages. Violence between partisans is very common and control over the polls by the governing party often results in the exclusion of the opposition. In addition, the local military unit interacts as arbiter, partisan, and opponent with the political parties. On occasion districts have been divided into armed camps between military and civilians or between an alliance of the military and one party against the other party. One of the causes of Villeda Morales impotence in imposing order and implementing many reform programs between 1957 and 1963 was his inability to gain military support of his party at the local level. On the o hand, one of the strengths of the López Arellano government was its support by a Nationalist party-military coalition.[22]

El Salvador

During popular uprisings in 1931 the Salvadorian military discovered a new role and forged a new ruling structure for itself and El Salvador's coffee planter oligarchy. Whether through the strong-arm dictatorship of General Maximiliano Hernández Martínez, who ruled between 1931 and 1944, or the political party that ruled after 1948, the Salvadorian military has controlled the instruments of government in order to maintain public order and permit the expansion of the Salvadorian economy under the leadership of coffee planters and industrial entrepreneurs.

The military sees its organizational and coercive power as only one part of the necessary instruments of political rule. In 1950 military officers created a mass-based political party to organize and control the electorate. The relation between Salvadorian party leaders and masses clearly differentiates their official party from the political parties of their neighbors. The PLN of Costa Rica has sought to integrate the masses into the political system through their participation in the open electoral process. In Nicaragua Somoza's Liberal party leaders have ignored the rural masses, leaving control over them to the National Guard. The two Honduran parties are sustained in the rural areas by traditional patterns of identification, yet there is little organization beyond dispersed local factions and leadership cliques. The Salvadorians, in contrast, have attempted to balance widespread participation with central control over the direction and form of that participation through the Revolutionary Party of Democratic Unification (PRUD) before 1960 and the National Conciliation party (PCN) since then.[23] To implement their "controlled revo-

22. Of course, such a coalition, while aiding the imposition of public order, does not guarantee the successful implementation of development programs, as will be demonstrated below.

23. PRUD was formed in 1950 by a military junta and the PCN was founded in 1961 by the civilian-military junta that replaced President Lemus. While its ideology is almost identical to PRUD and its member-

lution" they have intensely organized and propagandized their geographically concentrated rural poor against the threat of communist subversion while making some symbolic and substantive welfare policy gestures, e.g., minimum wage laws for farm workers and public housing.

To justify their one-party system, Salvadorian leaders often claim that they are modeling their style of rule after that of the Institutional Revolutionary party (PRI), the often-praised ruling party of Mexico. This analogy, despite its obvious appeal, does not hold up when the bases of support and structures of opposition in these two countries are compared. Unlike Mexico, El Salvador has not experienced a revolution that destroyed most of the landed oligarchy. As a consequence, the Salvadorian military leadership makes few attempts to control or tightly regulate the economic wealth of the country. Instead, it seeks to avoid destruction of the will of the landed oligarchy to produce, for in the official Salvadorian strategy of development the oligarchy's participation is essential to economic growth.

The PCN has also faced a more open challenge from its political opposition than has its Mexican counterpart. Because of military intimidation and their own abstention, opposition political parties did not occupy legislative seats between 1950 and 1964. Then under Colonel Julio Rivera the electoral law was reformed to permit greater opposition participation and intimidation was drastically reduced. In 1964 opposition deputies gained 20 of 52 legislative seats and increased their membership to 25 seats in 1968; by controlling over one-third of the unicameral legislature they have succeeded in blocking pieces of legislation, such as foreign loans, that require two-thirds congressional approval.[24] Demonstrating their strength primarily in urban areas, opposition parties also captured the mayorships of 8 of 14 provincial capitals in 1968. Thus the Salvadorian presi-

ship includes most of the same groups, the PCN claims to be a more widely based political organization.

24. Of the opposition parties the Christian Democrats were the most successful in the 1968 congressional elections gaining 19 legislative seats; they were followed by the Salvadorian Popular Party with 4 seats and the National Revolutionary Movement with 2 seats.

dent has confronted not only a patronage-ridden bureaucracy and elite obstruction of reform measures, but also an emerging electoral opposition.

Guatemala

In 1930 political power in Guatemala was consolidated in the very proficient hands of Jorge Ubico. Convinced of his country's incapacity for self-government, Ubico dominated it like a strict father. Forever active, venturing constantly into the countryside, and controlling the treasury like a tight family budget, Ubico gave constant attention to the small problems of his people, but did little to change the economic and social structure of his country.

The "revolutionary" regime that took power in 1945 provided a dramatic contrast to Ubico. This was particularly evident in its approach to political control. Ubico had relied on poor communications and a dispersed population to structure his rule. His power was hierarchical. Local and regional elites were allowed to rule throughout the country except when he personally intervened. The revolutionary regime, in contrast, created new forms of institutional identification between government and people: labor unions, peasant associations, cooperatives, and political parties. At the same time, the power of government was expanded and dispersed through the creation of such institutions as a development bank, a social security institute, a nationalized Central Bank and an agrarian reform agency.[25] Since the overthrow of the revolutionary government in 1954, the Guatemalan political leadership has changed often. The leader of the 1954 coup, Castillo Armas, was assassinated in 1957. His elected successor, Miguel Ydígoras Fuentes, was overthrown by a military coup in 1963, and the military government of Colonel Enrique Peralta was replaced by elected civilians in 1966.

The structure of political competition in Guatemala is strongly conditioned by the polarization of political forces caused by the

25. Richard N. Adams, *Second Sowing: Power and Secondary Development in Latin America* (San Francisco: Chandler Publishing Co., 1967), pp. 242–45.

revolutionary experience between 1944 and 1954. The dramatic ideological reversals that accompanied the rise and fall of the Arevalo and Arbenz regimes hardened the political cleavages in Guatemala. More than in any other Central American country, violent conflict between the radical left and the reactionary right has characterized the post-1954 Guatemalan political struggle. A clear indicator of post-1954 political instability is the rise and fall of Guatemala's political parties. New parties were formed in the mid-1950s after Castillo Armas outlawed all parties existing before 1954. Yet, by the presidential elections of 1966 the National Democratic Movement, Castillo Armas' official party, no longer existed nor did the Redención party that had elected President Ydígoras in 1958. Instead, the presidency was contested by Colonel Peralta's Institutional Democratic party (PID) that he formed in 1965, the National Liberation Movement (MLN) created in 1960, and the Revolutionary party first registered in 1958.

In summary, we can now recognize some of the salient characteristics of the Central American political systems and some of the opportunities and constraints that confronted the planners who entered each of them in the early 1960s. The Costa Rican system offered a firm tradition of administrative decentralization, a stable pattern of electoral competition, and a disbanded military establishment. The Nicaraguans, in contrast, offered a strong personalistic presidency which responded to few popular demands, manipulated the rules of political competition to its occupants' own advantage, and deftly employed a small but efficient military force. The Honduran system was dominated by a very combative, but decentralized two-party system and a military that has moved from periodic political intervention to direct political rule in coalition with one of the traditional political parties. El Salvador was firmly ruled by a mass-based political party guided by a coalition of the military and the economic oligarchy determined to preserve the nation's economic power structure. And, finally, Guatemala possessed the region's least stable leadership and most frequently changing and intensely conflicting political configurations as well as a military that rapidly expanded its desire and capability for political rule.

THE POLICY-MAKING PROCESS

As indicated above, I want to explain the planners' failure to achieve their investment objectives, their conflicts with presidents, and the impact of political structures on national development programs. To guide the search for explanations, a consistent conceptualization of the policy-making process is required. At best, it can serve only as a rough guide to the discovery of Central American policy-making patterns. In the chapters that follow I will focus on the following components of the policy-making process:

1. PATTERNS OF INTERACTION AMONG CENTRAL DECISION-MAKERS: Here I am concerned with the locus of influence over policy choices and the formal and informal patterns of interaction between planners and other decision-makers. I will focus particularly on the distribution of bargaining and command relationships among decision-makers; I want to know, for example, if presidents ignore, tolerate, or depend upon their planners when making development policy decisions. I also want to know if planners bargain with ministers to gain their cooperation or if they can command them. If the former, what techniques do they use? If the latter, from where do they derive their authority to command? These questions will be the subject of Chapter 3.

2. DEVELOPMENT POLICY OBJECTIVES AND INSTRUMENTS: Development policy is based upon assumptions about behavior and its environment and seeks to affect both. The specific goals of development policies are innumerable, for they reflect a gamut of human needs and aspirations. Nevertheless, most of these goals can be grouped into two types of policies which dominate decision-making in developing countries: resource mobilization and resource distribution.

The task of expanding national economic productivity has fallen largely onto the shoulders of governments in the developing countries. While the degree of public involvement varies substantially from country to country, its importance is undeniable in all cases. Principal among governmental functions is the acquisition and allocation of financial resources to aid the expansion and distribution of economic productivity. Guided by ideologies, economic models, or simply inertia, policy-makers select from a variety of fiscal, monetary, and regulatory policy instruments in seeking to fill their treasuries and allocate funds to numerous governmental activities.[26] It is the selection and use of such instruments that intensely concerns the new expertocracy which seeks to shape policy choices. They have made revenue, expenditure, and public investment policy the principal concerns of their planning efforts, for they recognize that the rational direction of the chaotic public sector is the first step in their pursuit of coherent development programs. I will focus on the planners' efforts to mobilize and allocate resources in Chapter 4.

3. POLICY IMPLEMENTATION: Implementation will be examined as the bureaucratic management of specific public investment policies. After a president and his planners initiate a policy, they must rely on administrators for the implementation of that policy. No matter how rational or compelling their programs, they are little more than paper documents if there exists no capable administrative apparatus to guide them to completion and deliver them to the appropriate clientele. If the coordination of fiscal policy choices was the planners' first priority in the 1960s, the creation of bureaucratic effectiveness was their second, for they quickly discovered the futility of pursuing the former without the latter. I will examine their impact on program implementation by focusing on their efforts to reshape bureaucratic structures and operations and to construct development projects in Chapters 5 and 6.

4. ENVIRONMENT OF POLICY INNOVATION: Numerous political and economic conditions may affect the planners' relations with presidents as well as their impact on the mobilization and allocation of resources. In seeking explanations for Central American

26. In my examination of policy instruments and objectives I draw on the framework developed in E. S. Kirschen, et al., *Economic Policy in Our Times* (Amsterdam: North Holland Publishing Co., 1964), Chaps. 1–7.

policy-making patterns it is necessary to examine some of those conditions by focusing on several normative and factual constraints on policy-making.[27] Normative constraints are products of the political power distributions found in the Central American countries and the norms and rules that are supported by these power structures. Such norms may dictate the acceptance or rejection of particular policy instruments and objectives. Certain tax measures or regulatory techniques, for example, may not be viable options for presidents because of the self-interested opposition of important power holders.

Factual constraints are even more clearly observable in Central American policy-making. Two of the most crucial are information and resources. To alter behavior policy-makers must understand it, and to understand it they require substantial information about human needs and desires. Such information, however, is very scarce in the policy-making processes of developing countries. In its absence policy-making often takes the form of quasi-experimental activity by ill-informed leaders who apply trial-and-error strategies to attain their policy objectives.

Increased information, however, may only sharpen the policy-maker's awareness of a second factual constraint: inadequate human and financial resources. The creation of an educated citizenry is a common policy objective in most developing countries, yet this objective is often pursued by governments which themselves lack skilled personnel. Similarly, governments often lack financial resources to implement costly development policies. They are frequently victims of the vicious circle of trying to expand the productivity of miniscule economies that do not yield sufficient revenues to support the public programs that are being used to stimulate that expansion.

The existence of these and similar constraints in the policy-making environments of developing countries is clearly apparent to even the casual observer. What is not so clear is their impact on the making of specific development policies. I want to know

27. For a general discussion of normative and factual constraints, see Joyce Mitchell and William Mitchell, *Political Analysis and Public Policy: An Introduction to Political Science* (Chicago: Rand McNally & Co., 1969), Chapters 9 and 10.

if constraints were perceived by Central American presidents and planners as insurmountable obstacles; if they were, how were policy choices shaped to account for them? If not, how did policy-makers manipulate or alter them? In Chapters 3 through 6 these constraints will be related to the behavior of planners and presidents, their mobilization and allocation of resources, and their implementation of development policies. Then, in Chapter 7, they will be used to explain the general patterns of policy innovation in Central America during the Development Decade.

2

The Policy Precedents
of the 1950s

CENTRAL AMERICAN ECONOMIC POLICY, like that of the rest
of Latin America, followed the lines of an outward-directed development model throughout the late nineteenth and early twentieth centuries.[1] Its concerns were reduced to the establishment
of basic requisites for the operation of the export economy and
to the use of taxation to tap a small proportion of the income
generated in the export-import sector, which provided the bulk
of the resources the state required in order to discharge its very
limited responsibilities. To follow this model, domestic policy-
making was sacrificed as policy choices fell under the domination
of the uncompromisingly automatic dictates of the gold standard,
which made internal events contingent upon the vicissitudes of
external trade.

The outward-directed model was the product of the doctrine
of economic liberalism that emerged victorious throughout Central America between 1870 and 1895. Once in power, the
Liberals removed the legal and structural impediments to the
expansion of the export economy. Central America's land tenure
system was the principal target of their liberation efforts. Tradi-

1. The outward-directed model is developed in ECLA, "Economic
Policy and Planning in Latin America," mimeographed, E/CN. 12/711
(Santiago, 1965).

tionally, large tracts of land had belonged to towns and to the Church and hence were excluded from private ownership. In pursuit of the export-economy policy goals, the Liberals secularized Church property, converted communal properties to private ownership, and facilitated the development of credit for new agricultural export activities. The growth of a new coffee-planter economic elite soon followed these economic policies. Almost simultaneously, foreign investments in transportation infrastructure were welcomed to the region as were foreign-owned banana plantations soon thereafter.[2]

While the Central American governments continued to view their export-oriented economic policy as the only conceivable development strategy, the larger Latin American states were already questioning the long-range utility of the outward-directed model. The halcyonic era which closed with World War I was followed by increasing export sector instability and consequent fluctuations in fiscal receipts, national income, exchange rates, monetary conditions, and rates of saving and capital formation. Initially, faith in the existing system prevailed as the post-1914 fluctuations were accepted as conditions inimical to the orderly conduct of Latin American economic life. But with the decline of foreign markets and investments during the depression of the 1930s came full recognition of the model's inherent weaknesses; there followed an intensive search for new policy alternatives.[3]

As a consequence of the economic and social problems deriving from the failures of the outward-directed development model, economic policy in such Latin American states as Argentina, Brazil, and Chile began to diversify by means of the incorporation of new aims and policy instruments which departed from the passive attitude of the past. Gradually, their economic policy improvisations reflected the emergence of what might be termed

2. Carlos M. Castillo, *Growth and Integration in Central America* (New York: Frederick A. Praeger, 1966), pp. 13–15.

3. An excellent discussion of this period in Latin American economic history is found in William P. Glade, *The Latin American Economies* (Princeton: D. Van Nostrand, 1969), pp. 362–70.

an inward-directed development model.[4] The new economic policy goals were centered on the stabilization of external trade and the alleviation of the impact of emergency conditions deriving from the depression. Policy measures were at first directed exclusively towards foreign trade but were later adjusted to stimulate internal economic activity as well. Initially, discriminatory import restrictions were imposed, nonexportable surpluses of goods were financed, and public works programs were launched in order to absorb unemployment solely in consideration of trade depression. Before long, however, the internal byproducts of these measures appeared in such forms as the encouragement of import substitution, the reinvigoration of production activities, the relief of the labor market situation, and the maintenance of income and demand.

The Central Americans, however, failed to follow the new policy shifts initiated by their Latin American neighbors to the south. Their very slight domestic markets afforded little opportunity for an internally oriented development strategy.[5] Consequently, they steadfastly clung to their traditional outward-directed economic policies and suppressed social protests that sought to alter this strategy in the 1930s.

By the end of World War II Central America's economic fortunes began to improve once again, justifying new faith in the outward-directed economic strategy. The first postwar decade, in fact, has been called "a period of almost unparalleled prosperity for most of the Central American countries, second only to the golden age of the traditional export economy between 1880 and 1900."[6] The price of coffee more than trebled between 1945 and 1954, foreign exchange earnings increased, and, through the use of this new income and large amounts of foreign reserves which had been accumulated during the war, imports were rapidly expanded to meet deferred needs and new demands. Yet,

4. On the inward-directed model also see ECLA, "Economic Policy and Planning in Latin America."
5. On the plight of the small Latin American countries see Glade, *The Latin American Economies*, p. 371.
6. Castillo, *Growth and Integration in Central America*, p. 48.

ironically, it was during this period of prosperity in the 1950s that Central American policy-makers began an intensive but cautious search for new development strategies. Unlike the Argentines, Brazilians, and Chileans, who improvised new policies in response to economic depression, the Central Americans embarked upon new policy initiatives while enjoying the luxury of a new wave of prosperity. Economic prosperity however, was more a catalyst for than a cause of their policy departures. More crucial was the rise of new political leaders who, armed with vague development ideologies, seized upon the new financial resources yielded by expanding national incomes and used them to support new development policies. These new reform leaders were nurtured on the optimism of new-found prosperity not the pessimism of tragic depression; consequently, their policy initiatives focused on the expansion of the productivity of existing economic institutions rather than the radical restructuring of their economies.

A CAUTIOUS BEGINNING

During the 1930s the Central American governments had been in the hands of the region's last generation of personalistic strong-arm presidents. Guatemala's Ubico, El Salvador's Hernández, Honduras' Carías, Nicaragua's Somoza, and, to a lesser extent, Costa Rica's Calderón, focused their rule on the maintenance of public order through the mediation and suppression of internal conflict. To the masses they had represented little more than traditional symbols of authority; to their small agrarian elites they were guarantors of an export-oriented economic policy. But to another minority of young military officers and civilian political aspirants they had become embarrassing autocrats who were completely unprepared to manage the complex issues raised by postwar prosperity and the embryonic demands for social reform. It was this new minority, stimulated by prosperity rather than adversity, that finally brought down the aging strongmen and replaced their rule with a new quest for productive development policies.

Central America's young postwar reformers came to power

with hopes and aspirations, not coherent programs and policy proposals. Their ideologies were eclectic, taken in bits and pieces from a variety of political and economic doctrines.[7] Their exposure to other Latin American countries, the United States, and Europe through travel and expanding communications had revealed Central America's embarrassing backwardness to them; yet, they had little comprehension of the complex causes and possible solutions to their plight. Instead, they first attacked the most abhorent manifestations of their backwardness, their traditionalist autocratic leaders, and then sought to imitate their more advanced neighbors through the updating of their governmental machinery and domestic policies.

In their attempts to catch up with their neighbors, Central America's new leaders initiated numerous economic policies that sought to stimulate economic development. Charles Anderson, in examining and comparing the policy initiatives of the 1950s has identified three distinct styles or policy mixes within the region.[8] Nicaragua and El Salvador pursued a "military conventional" approach to development policy, according to Anderson. In both governments the military exercised extensive policy-making power and its policy initiatives were directed at the expansion of the existing modern, market-oriented economic sector. In Nicaragua, as we have seen, most economic and political power was concentrated in the hands of the Somoza family. In contrast to their neighbors, the Somozas were not overthrown by a new cadre of reformers; instead, they incorporated the region's more conventional policy innovations into their rule after the assassination of the elder Somoza in 1956. True to form, they skillfully blended infrastructure and other public investment policies with the needs of their own agrarian enterprises. By focusing particularly on the development of lowland cotton production, they succeeded in guiding Nicaragua to the region's highest economic growth rate during the decade. In El

7. For detailed analysis of their ideologies see Charles W. Anderson, "Politics and Development Policy in Central America," *Midwest Journal of Political Science* 5 (November 1961): 332–50.

8. Charles W. Anderson, *Politics and Economic Change in Latin America* (Princeton: D. Van Nostrand, 1967), pp. 231–306.

Salvador the military's desire for order and the modern private sector's demand for official support blended together less tightly, but no less proficiently, than in Nicaragua. After its electoral victory in 1950, El Salvador's military-led governing party concentrated on infrastructure investment to support coffee and cotton production under the control of the nation's economic elite. Simultaneously, all radical political activity was suppressed while symbolic overtures were made in the area of social reform.

Costa Rica and Honduras followed an "alternation of conventional and reformist" policies. In essence, both sporadically exceeded the conventional stimulation of the modern sector and attempted to integrate their traditional, particularly rural, populations into the modern economic and political sectors. In Costa Rica José Figueres' National Liberation party sought to mobilize the rural poor into its organization: under Figueres' leadership in 1948 and 1949 and again between 1953 and 1958, the Costa Rican government wrote a new constitution, nationalized all banks, expanded social security programs, and increased public investments in order to expand production and more equitably distribute its benefits. While these policies persisted, official enthusiasm for them diminished when Costa Rica's conservatives returned to power in 1958. New leadership and reform policy came to Honduras later than Costa Rica with the presidency of Dr. Ramón Villeda Morales in 1957. Returning from exile in Costa Rica where he had closely observed Figueres' reform policies, Villeda sought to lead Honduras down a similar path. He soon discovered, however, that his task was much more difficult than that of Figueres. The brutal facts of Honduran underdevelopment, in contrast to Costa Rica's greater and better-distributed wealth, destroyed any illusions that similar policies would yield comparable results in the same period of time. Nevertheless, Villeda initiated new educational and public investment policies in an effort to draw Honduras out of its legacy of stagnation.

Lastly, there was Guatemala which added "radical discontinuities" to its alternation of conventional and reformist policies. To the Eisenhower administration, Guatemala's radical discontinuities were evidenced in its drift toward communism which the Central Intelligence Agency helped terminate by aiding the overthrow of the Arbenz regime in 1954. But in terms of economic policy-making, the Arevalo and Arbenz regimes which governed Guatemala from 1945 to 1954 vigorously tried to bring Guatemala up to date with the rest of the hemisphere. They created a development institute, a Central Bank, a social security program, and, like their neighbors, expanded infrastructure investments. Their principal "radical" initiative, which brought down the wrath of Guatemala's economic elite and the American government, was the Agrarian Reform Law of 1952 which led to the partial expropriation of United Fruit Company as well as of some national properties.

Although Central American leaders initiated their policies under the guidance of their vague, eclectic ideologies, they soon discovered appealing development strategies to guide and justify their policy choices in the early 1950s. Predictably, they found them when looking outward for assistance. They had come to view themselves, not always happily to be sure, as inescapably linked to external powers. They had been invaded by American Marines, their governments received financing from foreign banks, their economies were dependent on foreign markets, and the Americans had used them as a defense link with the Panama Canal during World War II. Quite naturally, they rejected the possible alternative of going it alone and searched the international community for intellectual and financial assistance. There they found two useful development strategies: the first, which we term orthodoxy, aided their cautious initiatives of the early 1950s; the other, termed neo-orthodoxy, offered a gamut of policy alternatives from which the Central Americans later selected their policy initiatives during the late 1950s and early 1960s.[9]

The Central American leaders' search for a new development strategy in the early 1950s was limited by some important economic and political assumptions. First, with the possible exception of the Guatemalans, they viewed themselves as alternatives to radical, particularly communist, regimes. Second, they

9. The terms orthodoxy and neo-orthodoxy are taken from Glade, *The Latin American Economies*, Chaps. 11, 12.

desired political stability; for some this required an expansion of political participation, but for all it included the firm organization and control of new political participants within structures supportive of the new leadership. Third, they recognized their dependence upon those entrepreneurs already active in the modern economic sector for continued economic expansion and acknowledged most of the policy claims of their productive economic elites as the price that they had to pay for stable economic growth. And fourth, as a corollary to their tolerance of their economic elites, they sought to improve the welfare of their poorer majorities by means of sharing some of the benefits of new growth rather than the radical redistribution of existing wealth. The product of these assumptions, they recognized, was gradual rather than dramatic economic development. Fortunately for Central American policy-makers, the costs and benefits of the orthodox development strategy conformed to these policy premises. In fact, the blend was almost perfect. Neither proposed radical change nor exacted high economic or political costs, yet both supported the expansion of production and the improvement of Central American welfare.

What I have termed the orthodox strategy is really an ideal type which combines numerous development policy objectives and measures, most of which were applied in Central America. It shares great continuity with the outward-directed model discussed above and therefore was very appropriate to the small Central American states that could not apply the inward-directed model followed by the larger Latin American states after 1930. The orthodox strategy was composed of three basic elements: a continuing effort to foster the growth of primary industries and export earnings; a concern with the development of infrastructure; and the promulgation of measures designed to create an investment climate capable of attracting foreign capital with all of its ancilliary benefits.[10] These objectives were grounded on the assumption that available Latin American resources were insufficient for attaining an acceptable rate of growth. Conse-

10. Ibid., p. 377.

quently, the aim of development policy should be that of augmenting domestic-factor supplies with resources generated by the operations of the external sector. The specific policies recommended by this strategy usually concentrated on increasing the output of products which depend mainly on employment of the region's relatively abundant labor and land factors. In practice, policy proposals have focused on transportation, communication, and power development, on fiscal reform to manage funds invested in projects that aid collateral private agricultural and industrial investments, and on agricultural development through the distribution of improved technology.[11] The congruence of these policies with the desires of Central American leaders is readily apparent. In applying them, their principal task was the selection of policy priorities for the distribution of their scarce public revenues.

The orthodox strategy was not discovered by chance, but was offered to Central America by foreign advisory missions that were invited to the region after the reformers took power. The most influential of these were the missions of the International Bank for Reconstruction and Development (IBRD) and the International Monetary Fund (IMF). In 1950 the Guatemalan government requested an IBRD mission to recommend economic policy guidelines. The following year Nicaragua received a similar mission, El Salvador welcomed a United Nations mission, and Costa Rica was examined by a group from the Twentieth Century Fund.[12] The Guatemalan study was somewhat superficial and was ignored by President Arbenz, who considered it too conservative for his reform-minded administration. Eventually, however, it served to guide the Castillo administration that overthrew him in 1954. In Nicaragua, in contrast, Anastasio Somoza warmly received the Bank report since its recommenda-

11. Ibid., pp. 371–98.
12. See Stacy May, et al., *Costa Rica: A Study in Economic Development* (New York: Twentieth Century Fund, 1952); IBRD, *The Economic Development of Guatemala* (Baltimore: Johns Hopkins University Press, 1952); IBRD, *The Economic Development of Nicaragua* (Baltimore: John Hopkins University Press, 1953).

tions on road construction and lowland agricultural development conformed with his desire to expand agricultural production without sacrificing his control over the Nicaraguan economy.[13]

The application of the orthodox strategy in Central America was strongly encouraged by the financial assistance offered by the agencies to aid the implementation of their policy proposals. Foreign financial assistance clearly appealed to the Central American leaders in the early 1950s. It supplied the foreign exchange needed for expensive development projects and its short-run costs were very low while its benefits—observable development projects—appeared quite high. Moreover, it was believed that in the long run the region's continuous economic growth would support the repayment of the loans. Stimulated by their new-found optimism, Central American presidents committed themselves for the first time to a gamut of new development projects and accepted the extensive financial obligations that such projects demanded. In the years that followed, their development policy commitments increased and so did their financial dependence on foreign assistance, for, as their economic fortunes declined in the late 1950s, they had nowhere to turn for support of their programs except to their new foreign benefactors.

The development assistance offered to Central America in the 1950s came primarily from the World Bank and the United States government and found its way into numerous productive investments. With loans from the World Bank's IBRD the Guatemalans built their Atlantic Highway, the Salvadorians constructed their Coastal Highway and Rio Lempa hydroelectric project, the Nicaraguans built numerous lowland roads, and the Hondurans connected their capital, Tegucigalpa, with the Inter-American Highway. The similiarity of the foreign-financed projects is no coincidence: international agencies selected transportation and power projects as their principal development targets throughout the region.

While the public investment policies stimulated by the foreign

13. John F. McCamant, *Development Assistance in Central America* (New York: Frederick A. Praeger, 1968), pp. 56–60.

missions met with small-scale, yet impressive success, their attempts to reshape Central America's policy-making processes through the introduction of economic planning were dismal failures. In fact, they were doomed from the beginning. The IBRD experts, although firm advocates of more rational policy-making, made only token attempts to create planning machinery. To be sure, Nicaragua in 1953, Guatemala in 1954, and Honduras in 1955 dutifully created planning agencies as requested by the missions.[14] But the planning agencies were staffed primarily with IBRD personnel who, when they departed in the late 1950s, left nearly empty offices behind. No public investment programs were prepared by the Nicaraguans and Hondurans in the late 1950s; only Guatemala made some effort at program creation after the IBRD departure.

It would be an exaggeration to view the attempts at planning during the 1950s as precursors of planning in the succeeding decade, for there was a sharp discontinuity between the two efforts. Only three of the five countries created planning agencies and two of those ceased to operate before the end of the decade. More important, very few development-policy technicians were trained and employed to assure development-policy continuity. Central American presidents had perceived no need for planning and, quite naturally, gave it no support after its creation by foreigners. Against this background, the emergence of the planners in the early 1960s can be seen as a new attempt to reshape Central American policy-making processes. It came not merely as an extension of the orthodox strategy, but as a response to new economic problems and a search for new policy instruments.

REGIONAL INTEGRATION: AN ALTERNATIVE TO DEVELOPMENT PROGRAMMING

As we have seen, the desire to escape from the outward-directed strategy produced numerous policy innovations in the

14. Nicaragua, Decreto Num. 6, febrero 1953; Guatemala, Decreto Num. 132, noviembre 1954; and Honduras, Decreto Ley Num. 40, febrero 1955.

larger Latin American states after 1930. This phenomenon had
not gone unnoticed in Central America, although there was little
official support for its replication anywhere in the region. Nevertheless, a small minority of Central Americans, particularly those
concerned with economic policy-making, began in the early
1950s to study other Latin American policy experiments in
search of innovations that might be useful in the region. While
their presidents were turning to the IBRD for assistance, they
sought inspiration and insight in the new neo-orthodox development strategy propagated by the Economic Commission for
Latin America (ECLA) which the United Nations had created
in 1948. Their faith in this multi-national instructor in political
economy was not misplaced, for eventually they acquired from
it the new policy insights that were to guide Central American
policy-making throughout the 1960s.

The Economic Commission for Latin America is an unusual
international organization, for it has fashioned a cohesive per-
sonality and a distinctive development ideology.[15] Its ideology
or doctrine is largely the work of ECLA Secretary General Dr.
Raul Prebisch, who initially expressed it publicly in an ECLA
pamphlet in 1950 entitled *The Economic Development of Latin
America and Its Principal Problems.* In essence, Prebisch succeeded in providing a comprehensive justification of the inward-
directed development model that had emerged incrementally
from the pragmatic responses of policy-makers in the larger Latin
American states. His most important contributions were a hard-
hitting analysis of Latin America's principal economic problem
and suggestions of some possible means of coping with it.

Although volumes have been written on it, Latin America's
basic development problem can be described quite briefly, according to Prebisch. Latin America, as a producer of food and
raw materials, is part of the world's "periphery" that suffers
from an "asymmetry" in its economic relations with the nations
of the industrial "center." Latin America's terms of trade with

15. For a brief summary of ECLA's early history see Albert Hirschman, "Ideologies of Economic Development in Latin America," in Hirschman, ed., *Latin American Issues* (New York: Twentieth Century Fund,
1961), pp. 12–23.

the industrial countries had been declining and would continue to do so, for, gradually but persistently, its industrial imports were becoming more expensive while its income, and with it foreign exchange, from food and raw product exports were not expanding at equivalent rates. Thus, unless many conditions drastically changed, the Latin American countries were, according to Prebisch, doomed to economic decline; the outward-directed development model, quite simply, had failed.

Having warned Latin America of its plight, Prebisch boldly suggested some remedies. First, and foremost, he called upon the Latin American governments to undertake new responsibilities in the promotion of economic development. Most governments, of course, had been increasing their responsibilities since 1930, but that did not satisfy Prebisch. He was concerned with the form and direction of government involvement in the economy. In a 1953 ECLA pamphlet entitled *An Introduction to the Technique of Programming*, he rejected the pragmatic poking and prodding of the economy so common in Latin America; to replace this unproductive policy-making style he urged the application of detailed programming to all government economic policy-making. While he denied that he was advocating rigid state control of the economy, he was convinced that "without state action to call for the correct amount of investment and to direct it into the proper channels, the Latin American economies would make numerous wrong decisions."[16] The task of programming was by no means simple nor was it familiar to most Latin American policy-makers. Included among its techniques were the creation of medium- and long-term aggregate and sectoral projections of economic growth based on relevant theoretical and empirical knowledge, the setting of growth targets and priorities, the creation of long-range public investment programs, and the application of program budgeting to guide the implementation of public policies.

ECLA officials comprehended the difficulty of applying programming techniques within the antiquated, traditional policy-making structures of the Latin American countries, hence, rather

16. Quoted ibid., p. 18.

than demanding the creation of national planning agencies, they sought to influence each government through more subtle means. Their strategy was simply the product of their recognition that the long-range success of programming required the enthusiastic support of political leaders within each regime. Such support would emerge, ECLA officials believed, only after political leaders were taught to recognize the benefits of programming. As a first step, they offered to send teams of ECLA economists to design development programs for each country. Although they were not always warmly received and their proposals were often ignored, these ECLA teams succeeded in completing studies of most of the larger Latin American economies by 1960. As a complementary measure, ECLA created the Latin American Institute for Development Planning to train Latin American government economists and engineers in the techniques of programming. By 1960 the Institute had trained 112 technicians who returned to their respective countries to staff ministries and planning agencies.[17]

Through its ideology, country studies, and training programs ECLA introduced new elements to the Latin American policy-making processes. They publicly identified the causes of the economic problems that had frustrated Latin American policy-makers for two decades and they clothed their discoveries with a concise and coherent theory that satisfied the nationalistic sentiments of many Latin American leaders. More important in the long run, they contributed to the development of a new expertocracy throughout Latin America. As might have been expected, their graduates were not always welcomed by their own political leaders, yet, with few exceptions, they were tentatively admitted to national bureaucracies throughout the hemisphere. As their numbers increased in the late 1950s, they shifted the locus of the new ECLA policy analysis from the conference tables and classrooms of ECLA headquarters in Santiago, Chile, to the capitals of Latin America, where the ECLA doctrines received a severe testing during the 1960s.

17. Only 19 of those trained before 1960 were Central Americans; the relative lack of Central American participation is the product of the Central American failure to accept planning until well into the 1960s.

While ECLA's programming techniques made impressive strides in some Latin American governments during the 1950s, they were totally ignored in Central America. Programming was simply passed by as the Central Americans rushed to grasp Prebisch's second major policy proposal: industrialization through the economic integration of Latin America. Prebisch originally offered the doctrine of economic integration as a means of resolving the economic problems of the larger Latin American states, not those of Central America. It is therefore one of the more interesting ironies that, of all Latin Americans, the Central Americans gave the integration doctrine its most enthusiastic support and thorough application.

Regional economic integration was offered by ECLA to deal with the difficulties which arose when underdeveloped countries entered the process of industrialization in isolation. By combining their markets, Latin American countries could overcome the principal obstacle to their industrialization—deficient internal demand. This would be achieved, it was argued, through a series of regional agreements leading from the abolition of internal tariffs and the creation of common external tariffs to the eventual free movement of labor and capital within a common market.[18] While many Latin American leaders viewed the doctrine with a detached curiosity, a small group of Central Americans amazed most of their neighbors by not only studying the doctrine carefully, but also by initiating a series of decisions that soon led to wide-ranging regional accords.

In retrospect, the sequence of decisions leading to the creation of the Central American Common Market appears to conform to a textbook model. In 1950 ECLA urged all Latin American countries to formulate development programs taking into ac-

18. On the theory of regional integration and its application to Central America see: Castillo, *Growth and Integration in Central America*; Roger Hansen, *Central America: Regional Integration and Economic Development* (Washington: National Planning Association, 1967); Joseph Nye, Jr., "Central American Regional Integration," *International Conciliation*, no. 562 (March 1967); and Philippe Schmitter, *Central American Integration: Spill-Over, Spill-Around or Encapsulation?* (Berkeley: University of California Institute of International Studies, 1971).

count regional integration. Soon thereafter, Central America's Ministers of Economy asked for ECLA's elaboration of the regional integration concept and ECLA responded in 1951 with an invitation to the Ministers to form an Economic Cooperation Committee to study the matter under the tutelage of advisors from ECLA's new office in Mexico City. The Committee then held five meetings between 1952 and 1957 at which integration studies were presented, areas of common agreement were mapped out, and the drafting of regional treaties was begun. Under the pressures of a post-1957 economic depression throughout the region the agreements of the previous seven years were consolidated in 1959 into the region's first integration treaty. The Multilateral Treaty of Free Trade and Central American Economic Integration, ratified by all Central American states but Costa Rica, created a free trade list of 200 items and outlined integration objectives to be achieved by 1968. There followed the Treaty of Economic Association between El Salvador, Guatemala, and Honduras in 1960 which, as a product of dissatisfaction with the Multilateral Treaty, attempted to accelerate the pace of economic integration. Finally, all states but Costa Rica, which joined in 1963, ratified in June 1961 a General Treaty of Central American Economic Integration which endorsed the free trade agreements of the Treaty of Economic Association and established an institutional structure composed of a Central American Economic Council, an Executive Council, and a Permanent Secretariat.

Throughout all of the Committee discussions that preceded the first integration treaty in 1959 one item was conspicuously missing. There is no evidence of any further consideration of national development planning after ECLA's initial request in 1951 for "the formulation of development programs taking integration into account."[19] It was as if the Ministers had thrown

19. A close examination of major Committee documents reveals no discussion of the planning issue. See the Committee meeting reports: Naciones Unidas, "La integración económica de Centroamérica," mimeographed, E/CN. 12/194 (20 junio 1950); E/CN. 12/275 (16 junio 1951); E/CN. 12/AC. 17/37 (16 octubre 1953); also United Nations, "Progress Report on the Central American Economic Integration Programme,"

out the bathtub to save the baby from drowning. In fact, something like this was the case. The Ministers of Economy and their ECLA advisors intentionally ignored the issue of development planning, leaving it to the very meager efforts of the IBRD, and concentrated instead on the task of regional economic integration. This deliberate choice of only one part of ECLA's neo-orthodox strategy merits some explanation.

The explanation must begin with the Central American scenario in 1950. In the Ministries of Economy of the five countries there emerged a handful of economists who, almost alone, had become skeptical of Central America's development potential under existing conditions. While impressed with the favorable world market for their primary product exports, they were concerned about the continuing predominance of agriculture in their economies and about their stagnating traditional sectors composed primarily of subsistence farming. Unlike some of their political superiors who were temporarily blinded by their short-run optimism, the economists were pessimistic about long-term development under these conditions. Unfortunately, the inward-directed development strategies that were emerging in some parts of Latin America offered them little help in dealing with these problems for they appeared inappropriate to the tiny Central American countries. Then, quite unexpectedly, they were offered new opportunities to solve their development problems when ECLA agreed in 1951 to assist with economic programming and regional integration.

The ECLA offer contained threats as well as opportunities, forcing the Ministers to develop a policy strategy that would avoid the former while taking advantage of the latter. The principal threat came from ECLA's request for economic planning, while the opportunity was the offer to initiate economic integration. Planning was a threat because it required the application of new criteria and techniques in selecting national policy priorities. In essence, it proposed a restructuring of the policy-making pro-

mimeographed, E/CN. 12/431 (20 April 1967); and United Nations, "Report of the Central American Economic Cooperation Committee," mimeographed, E/CN. 12/552 (3 September 1959–13 December 1960).

cess of each Central American government by demanding that political leaders make policy choices based on the rational analysis of their economies' overall development rather than merely through bargaining with traditional power contenders. And, contrary to first impressions, the new leaders' development ideologies were not automatically receptive to planning simply because they had called for economic development. In fact, they had little to say about changing national decision-making patterns. Their vision of governmental responsibilities, as we have seen, was a narrow one that focused almost entirely on additional public investments in very obvious areas like highways, hydroelectric power, and communications. Under these conditions the Ministers, themselves uncertain of their role in these new regimes, were unwilling to challenge the traditional policy-making process. Instead, they selected the avenue of least resistance and concentrated on the region's economic integration.[20]

The Ministers' decision to pursue the path of least resistance is not surprising, for the contrivance of policy innovation often requires the circumvention of major political obstacles. What is surprising, however, is their choice of economic integration as the least difficult path to follow. It appears that they examined the two complementary policy instruments suggested by the ECLA neo-orthodox strategy, speculated about the reception of each by their political superiors, and concluded that the very complex process of integrating the economies of five sovereign states was more feasible than the application of economic planning within those states. In fact, the success of the former appeared to require the postponement of the latter. Thus, they made the unusual discovery that an innovation in the international system was more easily attainable than changes in national policy-making processes.

While their choice of integration is at first puzzling, a closer examination of the Central American environment reveals that it was quite logical, particularly when two dominant characteristics of the policy-making process are taken into account. It

20. This explanation of the choices made during the early stages of regional integration is drawn largely from interviews; see Note on Sources.

will be recalled from Chapter 1 that personalism in politics and the management of the economy by the private sector were identified as two characteristics of Latin American policy-making. Both are particularly evident in Central America. Therefore, when one considers the two ECLA development policy innovations within this context, it is clear that planning might be perceived as a serious threat to personalistic control and to the freedom of the well-entrenched private sector. Economic integration, on the other hand, initially brought only new visibility and dignity to national leaders who perceived themselves as pathfinding diplomats pursuing the traditional and noble goal of integration, and it encouraged the private sector's management of the expanding, integrated economies. When you add to these conditions the Ministers' belief that integration would yield the increased economic productivity desired by Central Americans, their policy choice becomes quite compelling.

The singular pursuit of economic integration also offered several tactical advantages supporting its official acceptance that were not shared by economic planning. Integration was, or at least could be made to appear, a technical and, therefore, non-controversial approach to development. In arguing for integration in their respective cabinets the ministers had the initial advantage of superior technical competence that was not shared by their political superiors. They employed their skills not only in disguising some issues but, more important, in convincing their listeners that integration was purely a matter of technical, nonpolitical decision-making.[21] In this way the Ministers carefully avoided the type of controversy that would have surrounded their attempt to create national planning machinery.

The Ministers were also supported by Central America's historical attachment to the idea of regional union. As one Central American observer has noted, "an awareness of the need to reestablish the Central American union survived the disintegration of the federal republic [1824–1842] and has been shared by the five governments to the present time."[22] Most previous attempts

21. Nye, "Central American Regional Integration," pp. 19–20.
22. Castillo, *Growth and Integration in Central America*, p. 67.

at union were dismal failures and many of the conditions that caused their demise, e.g., personal rivalries, crude nationalism, and imbalances in regional development, also existed in 1950. Nevertheless, the Ministers skillfully exploited the ideal of union as a normative goal in selling integration to their political superiors.[23]

The economic and political costs of integration also appeared quite low at the beginning. Little power was actually granted to regional institutions and initially the fiscal loss due to tariff reductions appeared small.[24] More important, economic integration demanded few sacrifices by Central America's powerful landed oligarchies. The technicians keenly recognized that the integration program would avoid the zero-sum implications of such other paths to development as unpopular agrarian reform by means of its expansion of markets, industrial production, and employment. Those political leaders who remained unconvinced by integration's technical noncontroversiality soon found much reassurance in these obvious low initial economic and political costs.

Finally, integration as a development strategy conformed to Central America's traditional development perspective. The countries' leaders had always looked outward for solutions to their economic problems. They had become linked to foreign economies and, in searching for new development strategies, they had looked to international organizations and foreign governments. The addition of economic integration to their list of policy instruments appeared to many only a further extension of their tradition of applying external solutions to internal problems.

By 1960 it was clearly apparent that the Ministers of Economy had adroitly avoided changing the traditional rules of the national policy-making process while establishing an institutional framework for the implementation of their regional development strategy. They had cleverly adopted only that part of ECLA's

23. On their efforts to sell the idea of integration to political leaders see: James D. Cochrane, *The Politics of Regional Integration: The Central American Case*, Tulane Studies in Political Science, vol. 12 (New Orleans: Tulane University Press, 1969), pp. 52–53.

24. Nye, "Central American Regional Integration," p. 33.

neo-orthodox doctrine that was acceptable within Central America's politico-economic environment and, as the decade ended, they looked forward to reaping the benefits of their initiatives through the expansion of integration in the 1960s.

A DECADE OF PUBLIC INVESTMENT

Even though development planning did not become a policy-making technique in Central America during the 1950s, the region's presidents nevertheless did embark on a new era of development policy-making.[25] They did so, however, on their own terms, using familiar fiscal policy instruments to expand public expenditures and to allocate public investments to new development projects. Their efforts were sometimes confused and their policies inconsistent, yet they succeeded in initiating a gamut of new development policy commitments that firmly bound their successors during the following decade.

Fiscal policy choices are excellent indicators of changes in development policy-making. New development programs require appropriations taken either from existing programs or from additional revenues. Each new policy initiative is therefore accompanied by a series of presidential choices involving the implicit or explicit allocation of policy priorities. For example, a presidential commitment to governmental construction of a new highway does not stop with the president's expression of an intention to initiate the project. He must also rate the project in his list of priorities and, assuming a scarcity of funds, he must select a means of financing the additional national and foreign exchange costs of the project. These requirements may force a reevaluation of existing expenditure priorities and an examination of revenue policy. More likely, however, they will produce only a hasty scrambling to find short-term financing either in national or international financial markets or through new tax-

25. The following discussion is based on: Anderson, *Politics and Economic Change in Latin America*, pp. 231–306; Naciones Unidas, Cepal, *La política tributaria y el desarrollo económico en Centroamérica* (Mexico City, 1956), passim; interviews with Central American planners cited in Note on Sources.

ation. Whatever the series of choices, they will reflect the policy goals and policy-making style of a particular regime. Moreover, fiscal policies also serve as convenient and useful objects of comparative policy analysis, permitting the longitudinal analysis of policy-making within one country and between countries.

Central America's new postwar leaders did not find their policy-making environment particularly hospitable to new development policy initiatives. To be sure, they accurately perceived a rising public demand in their urban centers for an expansion of development projects. Yet, against this they had to weigh a policy legacy that appeared quite hostile to their objectives. Their Central Banks, well aware of the potentially disastrous effects of inflation on the balance of payments of their small export economies, traditionally adhered to tight credit policies that had forced presidents to keep public investment within the narrow bounds of existing resources and taxes. Consequently, the principal functions of government had long been limited to only the maintenance of order, the preservation of the export economy, and the occasional provision of patronage. These responsibilities were implemented with balanced budgets and very little growth in public expenditures. Equally important, the Central American governments depended on very inflexible import and consumption taxation for nearly all government revenues. Public expenditures, therefore, were inexorably linked to foreign trade and subject to its inherent instability. Finally, Central American leaders were forced to look inward, not outward, for new financing in 1950. The financing offered by international agencies was limited to the foreign exchange costs of only a few projects and most of it was not disbursed until the latter half of the decade; the massive financing offered by the Alliance for Progress would not arrive for another decade, so the Central Americans were initially very much dependent on their own resources.

In addition to their conservative fiscal policy tradition, the region's presidents confronted numerous technical problems in the immediate postwar period. As a result of the war, there was a scarcity of capital equipment. Moreover, Central American public administration, which had never before been called upon

selected imports, and alcoholic beverages in order to
public investments and control inflation. El Salvador, in
, followed a more conservative policy. From the begin-
w expenditures were matched first with small increases
e export taxes and later with a modest increase in the
tax in 1951. In addition, the Salvadorians employed two
BRD loans to cover the foreign exchange costs of their
ncipal development projects.

a Rica and Nicaragua struggled to escape the constraints
rigid tax structures after initiating new investments in
y 1950s. Both suffered from postwar inflation caused by
ing government expenditures and the use of national bank
to finance them. To this were added foreign exchange
n 1949 and 1950. Austerity programs during 1950 and
helped ease these conditions, but not until new tax mea-
were promulgated were they able to initiate new develop-
projects. In 1949 the Costa Ricans substantially increased
axation of foreign banana companies; an ad valorem tax
fee was added in 1950, and import taxes were increased
4. Similiarly, the Nicaraguans enacted a coffee tax in 1950
modest income tax in 1952 with rates ranging from 4 to
cent.

nduras, because its government was even poorer than those
neighbors, seized upon tax reform as the prerequisite for
xpenditures. An income tax was promulgated in 1949
ng largely on the foreign banana companies and, following
osta Rican and Nicaraguan examples, the Hondurans in-
d taxes on nonessential imports in 1955.[27]

1955 all of the Central American governments had suc-
d in quietly modifying their revenue policies through minor,
ot inconsequential, tax reforms. Their efforts produced the
ance as well as the familiar symbols of change, for between
and 1954 tax revenues at constant prices increased by 150
nt in Costa Rica, 100 percent in El Salvador and Nica-
, 78 percent in Honduras, and 66 percent in Guatemala.[28]

The preceding three paragraphs summarize data found ibid.,
n.
Ibid., p. 23.

to perform major developmenta
pared for the management of lar;

But despite all of these fisc.
Central American presidents exp
stantially between 1947 and 19
concentrating their policy initiati
that could be managed largely by
for example, increased its total p
cent at constant prices during tl
Nicaragua with 98 percent, Costa
dor with 83 percent, and Guatem.

Quite naturally, one must ask
fiscal policy traditions, the Centi
ceeded in increasing their expendi
is found, to a large extent, in their a
structures that produced enough ir
tures. To aid them they had a fa
beginning of the decade which yi
export tax revenues. But these re
not sufficient to cover all new expe
some careful tinkering with tax :
revenue sources. The latter provides
cautious policy-maker who, when u
revenues from his nation's leading e
subtly chips away at them to genera
curring their wrath.

Guatemala and El Salvador repres
the use of minor tax reforms to sustai
Initially, Guatemala's revolutionary
penditures without altering tax structu
it began to face large deficits that had
ing from the national banking systen
turn, caused substantial inflation an
which soon exhausted foreign exch;
1951 the government responded by i

exports.
sustain
contras
ning ne
in coffe
income
large II
two pri

Cost
of thei
the ear
increas
credit
crises i
1951 h
sures v
ment p
their t:
on cof
in 195
and a
18 pei

Ho
of its
new e
focusi
the C
crease

By
ceede
but n
subst:
1947
perce
ragu:

27
passir
28

26. Naciones Unidas, Cepal, *La política*
nómico en Centroamérica, p. 5.

Nevertheless, the tax reforms, while yielding increased revenues, failed significantly to alter the region's overall tax structures (see Table 2.) Although new income taxes, especially those directed

TABLE 2
Tax Structures in 1947 and 1954 Compared

	Income %		Exports %		Imports %		Internal Consumption %	
	1947	*1954*	*1947*	*1954*	*1947*	*1954*	*1947*	*1954*
Costa Rica	4.8	14.0	1.5	5.6	64.3	57.4	22.3	16.5
El Salvador	5.9	6.8	14.3	29.5	48.7	34.1	21.2	17.0
Guatemala	10.7	6.2	9.1	19.0	36.7	38.0	29.4	24.2
Honduras	1.0	20.6	2.4	2.8	59.8	50.0	31.0	22.1
Nicaragua	—	4.9	3.1	5.3	59.5	61.6	28.1	20.6

Source: Naciones Unidas, Cepal, *La política tributaria y el desarrollo económico en Centroamérica* (Mexico, 1956), pp. 24–25.

at foreign enterprises, were added to existing tax policy instruments, most of the reforms merely expanded existing indirect taxes. In pursuing this path of limited reform the Central American leaders chose the only politically viable strategy available to them; but in doing so, they left their rigid tax structures essentially intact—to the eventual frustration of the development planners of the 1960s.

Having examined the revenue side of Central American fiscal policy, we can now return to public expenditures as an indicator of development policy change in the 1950s. Of interest is not only the initial growth of expenditures, but also their performance under conditions of prosperity before 1957 and depression thereafter.

Current central government expenditures increased by an annual rate of 6.9 percent between 1950 and 1955 throughout Central America, reflecting the expansion of governmental operations and the creation of new executive agencies. Most indicative of development policy expenditures, however, are the public investments of the five governments. As we know, most public investments during the decade were allocated to the expansion of economic infrastructure although some social infrastructure was also produced.[29]

The Central American public investment pattern in the 1950s is quite clear; it was a decade of a dramatic rise and an equally dramatic decline in public expenditure growth. The explanation for the decline is also apparent: with a fall in export prices in 1957 came falling national income and with it diminished public revenues. This revenue decline during a period of increasing current expenditures yielded little public saving for use in public investment. Additional internal borrowing offered some compensation, but Central America's conservative fiscal traditions and its limited internal credit prevented extensive use of this compensatory alternative. Thus throughout Central America revenues that had expanded at an average annual rate of 8.6 percent between 1950 and 1955 declined to a growth rate of 4.3 percent between 1955 and 1960. As a result, public investments that had grown steadily until 1957 declined dramatically thereafter.

Public investment by the five governments is compared longitudinally in Fig. 1. The failure of the five governments to sustain their initial investment growth rate is clearly evident in the common decline of investment between 1957 and 1959. Only Guatemala's conspicuous growth between 1954 and 1957 deviates from the general pattern. As is often the case with unusual fluctuations in public expenditures, the Guatemalan phenomenon was caused by a unique event. The Guatemalan government enjoyed a resource windfall when the United States government, in an attempt to shore up the Castillo regime that it had aided in the overthrow of the leftist Arbenz, poured loans and grants into the country between 1955 and 1957. The flow was not sustained long enough, however, to compensate for the revenue decline after 1957.

As the decade closed, the once optimistic and now frustrated Central American leaders were searching for the means of recovering from depression and regaining the prosperity and levels

29. These data, and those in succeeding paragraphs, are from SIECA, *Resumen de los programas centroamericanos de inversiones publicas* (Guatemala, 1965), passim.

FIGURE 1   Central American Public Investments

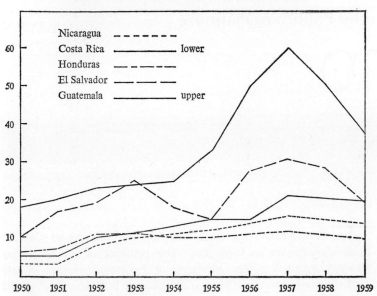

Source: SIECA, *Resumen de los programas centroamericanos de inversiones públicas* (Guatemala, 1965), p. 3. (Figures are in millions of U S dollars at current prices.)

of public investment reached in 1957. After surviving the familiar cycle of prosperity and depression in the 1950s, they sought the means for the better management of both, should they occur in the decade ahead. Their search was not in vain, as they were soon to discover. In 1961 they would join the Alliance for Progress and welcome its cascade of foreign advisors and financial assistance. Also in 1961 they would sign the General Treaty of Central American Economic Integration and would reap a short burst of economic expansion stimulated in part by the growth of intra-regional trade. Finally, they would witness a convergence of demands by Alliance administrators and Common Market technicians for the initiation of national economic planning and the application of comprehensive development programs.

3

The Politics of Planning

In retrospect, the final initiation of planning in Central America appears to have been the product of an ingenious strategy pursued by the Ministers of Economy. Aware of the difficulties of securing official acceptance of both integration and planning in the 1950s, they postponed the latter in order to secure a foothold through the creation of the former. After initiating integration, they had a new and more compelling justification for national planning; namely, the success of integration required it. Presidents, once committed to integration, could hardly refuse some gesture toward the creation of planning machinery when confronted by such compelling demands. The Ministers' timing also appears quite adroit, for, just as they made their demands, the new Alliance for Progress was making similiar demands and offering enticing financial rewards for the application of planning. In the end, both sets of demands combined to overwhelm Central American leaders and force their acceptance of new planning agencies and their corps of technicians.

The planners, however, now admit that the emergence of planning was not actually the product of such a calculating and well-managed strategy. There is little evidence that planning was consciously delayed simply to await the emergence of a compelling new justification for its acceptance. Nor was the creation of the Alliance predictable in the late 1950s. It is more plausible

that the Ministers' initial postponement of planning was indefinite. It was only after creation of the Common Market Secretariat
(SIECA) in 1961 that regional technicians, many of whom were
trained by ECLA, once again raised the issue. Where the Ministers were concerned with treaty creation, the SIECA technicians
focused on treaty implementation. Included among the new
treaties were plans for regional road and telecommunications
programs, proposals for fiscal policy coordination, and agreements on monetary and tariff policy harmonization. But to
implement these programs the technicians discovered not well-
prepared national governments, but public works ministries dominated by spoils politics, impotent budget offices that only ratified the budgetary power struggles of government agencies, and
Central Banks that jealously guarded their autonomous powers.
To cope with these conditions the SIECA technicians sought,
by means of the application of national planning, to impose
some kind of order on the five chaotic national policymaking
processes.[1]

If SIECA was the principal external initiator of national
planning, the Alliance for Progress was its major external catalyst.
The hastily contrived, multi-faceted Alliance agreement signed
by the Latin American governments at Punta del Este in August
1961, reflected the development policy hopes of much of the
Central American leadership that had come to power with the
reform movements of the 1950s. These leaders also embraced
it because it promised relief from the fiscal crises that had plagued
all Central American governments for three years before the
Punta del Este meeting. But in welcoming the Alliance's financial
assistance, the Central American leaders soon discovered that
they must also confront its requirements for social and economic
reform under the direction of national planning agencies.

The Alliance and the hemispheric agreements that immediately
preceded it were based on the recognition of its designers that
market indicators were inadequate to guide development and
that special measures were essential, given existing institutional

1. This explanation of the delays in the emergence of planning is
based on interviews with the officials involved; see Note on Sources.

structures, to resolve the disproportionalities of the historic patterns of growth in Latin America and to insure a socially desirable diffusion of the benefits of growth.[2] One of the principal measures recommended by the Alliance was development planning on national and hemispheric levels. To assist in the application of planning the Inter-American Committee of the Alliance for Progress (CIAP) was created in 1963 to make detailed annual evaluations of the planning operations and development strategies of each Latin American government and to coordinate international financing of their development programs. Since 1964 the annual CIAP reports have supplied the most penetrating analysis of Central American development planning and I will draw upon them in the discussion below.

After signing the Alliance charter at Punta del Este the Central American presidents eagerly awaited the international financial assistance that would soon reach their treasuries. In anticipation they legislated compliance with many of the Alliance requirements. Almost over night the sleepy planning agencies of Guatemala, Nicaragua, and Honduras were revitalized with new funding, additional personnel, and the task of creating new development plans; moreover, in 1962 and 1963 planning agencies were created for the first time in El Salvador and Costa Rica. Appearances were deceiving, however, for this compliance with Alliance requirements contained more form than effective policy as the presidents had little expectation, and in some cases little desire, that agrarian reforms, new welfare policies, and development planning would be effective. But, as they soon discovered, the fate of these innovations was not entirely in their own hands. Gradually, often to their displeasure, Central American presidents began to recognize that, once initiated, these new programs gathered both their own momentum and national and international sponsors who constantly pressed for their effective implementation. This is particularly true of planning which unleashed a new corps of national *técnicos* who expected and

2. William P. Glade, *The Latin American Economies* (Princeton: D. Van Nostrand, 1969), p. 509.

demanded presidential adoption and implementation of their development policy proposals.

THE RESHAPING OF POLICY-MAKING STYLE

The *técnicos* who staffed Central America's new planning agencies found not a set of coherent development policies but a heterogeneous patchwork of policies—relating to fiscal and monetary questions, agriculture, industry, welfare, and foreign trade—which dealt with problems in a piecemeal manner. Policy aims, moreover, were unclear and often contradictory. The planners immediately turned to the source of the problem, the policy-making processes that had yielded this confusion, and set about restructuring their antiquated practices. Their immediate task was the coordination of economic policy-making; this included the explicit definition and the predetermined compatibility of both their policy objectives and the instruments and machinery required for their implementation. To do this they set about drafting new development plans and, in their own words, "organizing an institutional system, which includes both the establishment of new agencies and the coordination of those that already exist, and the application of new procedures, approaches and outlooks at every administrative level."[3] In essence, they sought to reshape the content of development policy as well as the means of making and implementing it. In this chapter I will examine their impact on policy-making structure, while in Chapter 4 the focus will be on development policy content and in Chapters 5 and 6 on policy implementation.

The planners sought, in theory at least, to apply what Charles Lindblom has termed a synoptic concept of public problem-solving to the Central American policy-making processes. In its purest form the synoptic approach requires that the policy-maker: 1) pursue an agreed-on set of values; 2) clearly formulate the aims of policy in advance of choosing among alternative

3. ECLA, *Economic Survey of Latin America—1964* (New York, 1966), p. 329.

policies; 3) attempt a comprehensive overview of policy problems and alternative policies; 4) coordinate all policies; and 5) consider all economic variables and values.[4] The synoptic model is a noble ideal but it cannot be successfully applied to practical affairs, according to Lindblom. It fails as a useful model because it is not adaptable to the realities of problem-solving situations. For example, it is not adaptable to man's limited problem-solving capacities, to inadequate information, to the costliness of analysis, to the closeness of fact-value relationships, to the openness of the system of variables, and to the diverse forms in which policy problems actually arise.[5]

If we recall the description of the Latin American policy-making process presented in Chapter 1, it is clear that the synoptic techniques would encounter numerous specific obstacles if applied in Central America. The crucial question, however, is not the existence of inhospitable conditions, for they are obvious, but whether or not such conditions are amenable to change through the application of synoptic techniques. That is, can the planner alter enough conditions to permit his collecting sufficient information, his making rational choices, and his raising the levels of administrative performance, or must he simply adapt his techniques to these conditions? Lindblom argues that planners must significantly adjust their expectations and practices. His conclusion is not based on the analysis of Latin American conditions, but on the study of man and reality in general. The synoptic model is a cognitive impossibility, he argues, for no man or group of men can collect and interpret sufficient information to realize it.

Lindblom's finding has been applied to the planning process by Bertram Gross who, after editing a series of four monographs on economic planning in developing countries, concluded:

Central omnipotence and central omniscience are the two most widespread myths of national economic planning. Under the former some

4. David Braybrooke and Charles E. Lindblom, *A Strategy of Decision: Policy Evaluation as a Social Process* (New York: The Free Press, 1963), p. 38.
5. Ibid., pp. 48–55.

central authority is supposed to issue orders to government agencies, private enterprises, and individuals. Under the latter these orders are allegedly based on the findings of econometricians on the optimal allocation of resources. The two together yield a rational plan which is flexibly adjusted through "feedback information" to changing environmental circumstances.[6]

If the synoptic model is a myth, what then is the normal pattern of planning in most developing countries? Here again, Lindblom and his followers have a ready answer. The policy-maker's adjustment to his cognitive limitations produces a decision-making style of "disjointed incrementalism," which includes a practical comparison of policy alternatives only slightly deviating from the status quo, the consideration of only a limited variety of policy alternatives and consequences, the adjustment of objectives to feasible policies rather than vice versa, and a remedial, rather than comprehensive, orientation of analysis and evaluation.[7] In the competitive political environment these traits manifest themselves not through the imposition of an ideal plan on the public sector, as would be the case under the synoptic model, but through a process of mutual adjustment by planners, political leaders, ministers, private enterprises, and international agencies.[8]

Lindblom's arguments are primarily theoretical. One can, however, test their descriptive utility by examining planning in Central America. My primary concern is the planners' success in imposing the synoptic model on Central American policy-making. In particular, I want to know how well they have succeeded in reshaping decision-making processes. If in fact their efforts have not radically altered Central American policy-making styles, I want to know why they have failed.

6. Bertram M. Gross, "The Drifting Cloud of Guided Development," preface to John Friedmann, *Venezuela: From Doctrine to Dialogue* (Syracuse: Syracuse University Press, 1965), p. xiii.

7. Braybrooke and Lindblom, *Strategy of Decision*, pp. 83–106; see also Charles E. Lindblom, *The Intelligence of Democracy* (New York: The Free Press, 1965), Chaps. 1–5, for a more normative exposition of the "partisan mutual adjustment" concept.

8. Gross, "The Drifting Cloud," p. xiv.

PLANNERS AND PRESIDENTS

Although no particular model was followed by the Central American governments in creating their planning agencies, agency structures and operations were strongly influenced by the regional Joint Planning Mission (JOPLAN) created by SIECA. Like so many advisors to the Central American governments, the JOPLAN economists accepted the conventional wisdom that Central American presidents were strong political leaders. Consequently, they recommended that planning agencies be located within the offices of presidents in the hope that they would benefit from presidential support. They gambled that presidential support would be forthcoming, but they could hardly have done otherwise, for without presidential backing the agencies had little hope of success.[9] The five planning agencies also shared structural similarities resulting from JOPLAN influence. Within each planning system there was a national planning council composed of cabinet ministers and public bank directors and a technical planning agency which was responsible to either the council, the president or both. In practice, most of the responsibilities for plan design and management were allocated to the technical planning agencies.

Planning reached an important turning point in Central America in 1965. Although some of the governments had designed plans before that date, a concerted and coordinated planning effort began in 1965 with the creation of Five Years Plans for the 1965–69 period by all of the Central American governments. The Joint Planning Mission assisted in the design of the plans and assured their conceptual and methodological consistency. Soon afterwards the JOPLAN technicians departed from the five governments, leaving the national planners to struggle on their own. Each Five Year Plan they left behind contained a projection of macroeconomic goals and agricultural, industrial, and public investment programs. While the plans were oriented

9. This strategy was revealed in interviews with regional planners; see Note on Sources.

toward regional development, they proposed no fundamental changes in national economic or social structures.[10] As they had done since they had taken power, Central America's reform presidents accepted the distribution of economic and political power in their societies as given conditions that were not amenable to immediate change.

Before examining and comparing the national experiences, a brief introduction to the principal participants in the planning process is required.[11] The supporters of planning sought not only the creation of new decision-making procedures, but also the simultaneous alteration of the traditional behavior patterns of each government's key policy-makers. In addition, planning brought new actors and organizations into national policy-making processes as technicians and representatives of international agencies sought to assist presidents and their ministers.

The most important participants in the planning process were the Central American presidents. During the period under examination this group included Ydígoras, Peralta, and Méndez in Guatemala; Rivera and Sánchez in El Salvador; Villeda and López in Honduras; the Somoza brothers and Schick in Nicaragua; and Orlich and Trejos in Costa Rica. The introduction of planning confronted these men with a basic dilemma: how could they integrate planning into their policy-making processes without threatening traditional ministerial and private power contenders who had prospered as participants in traditional policy-making processes? Central American presidents, as we have seen, assumed the continuance of their political and economic power structure and made development policy in conformity with the demands of their countries' principal power contenders. The introduction of planning and its synoptic approach to decision-making threatened this traditional arrangement. And as international and foreign agencies entered the scene with their demands for planning in exchange for financial assistance, these threats to

10. SIECA, Misión Conjunta de Programación, *Resumen de los planes centroamericanos de desarrollo económico y social para el periódo 1965–1969* (Guatemala, 1965), pp. 1–3.

11. The following analysis of roles and dilemmas is drawn from both documents and interviews; see Note on Sources.

the traditional system were greatly intensified, to the frustration of the presidents.

The second group were the economists and engineers who staffed the technical planning agencies in each government. Like their colleagues in other Latin American governments, these *técnicos* tended to think of themselves as a new elite group that was "above politics."[12] Nearly all planners aspired to synoptic policy-making, and when asked about the causes of development policy shortcomings, they consistently pointed to political leaders who, they claimed, had selfishly disregarded the more "rational" policy alternatives. Most of the planners were young men in their thirties or forties who had received university degrees from their national universities and had done graduate work in the United States or Europe. The majority had also taken the ECLA planning course. In contrast to only 19 Central Americans who studied at ECLA between 1952 and 1960, 68 took the planning course between 1961 and 1968.[13] By 1965 each planning agency had at least 8 or 10 well-trained technicians who had gained their first planning experience by designing their 1965–69 Five Year Plans with the assistance of JOPLAN technicians. The most active leadership among them was supplied by José Antonio Palacios and José A. Andrade in Guatemala; Armando Baltazar Rivera and Guillermo Borja Nathan in El Salvador; Miguel Angel Rivera and Alvaro R. Mencía in Honduras; Antioco Sacasa Sarria and Edgar Sevilla Reyes in Nicaragua; and Fernando Mora in Costa Rica. Like the presidents they served, these men faced their own dilemma: how could they impose unwanted change on the policy-making process without forcing presidents into withdrawing their much needed support of planning? If they took their assignments seriously, they would have to challenge presidents and power contenders to alter their policy demands and behavior to conform with new methods of policy

12. The Central American planners responded similiarly to the *técnicos* described by Nathaniel Leff in his study of Brazilian policy-making, *Economic Policy-making and Development in Brazil 1947–1964* (New York: John Wiley and Sons, 1968), pp. 143–53.

13. ECLA, *Report on the Activities of the Latin American Institute for Economic and Social Planning*, E/CN.12/817 (Santiago, 1969), p. 20.

analysis and implementation. But if they did not take their work seriously, they would suffer the humiliation of having developed professional competence only to have used it as window dressing in support of presidential acquisition of international assistance.

The planners found an occasional ally in a third group of participants, the regional and international technicians who supported planning and development in Central America. SIECA expressed its support of planning through its JOPLAN mission. But like everyone else, SIECA technicians faced a dilemma. They were confronted by the problem of creating national planning agencies that were strong enough to influence national policy-making but not so strong that they could ignore SIECA's demands for the sacrifice of national interest in favor of regional policy coordination. International agencies, on the other hand, were primarily concerned with the efficient and effective application of financial assistance in support of development programs. But they too had a problem. They could encourage the creation and operation of planning agencies by making planning a prerequisite for financial assistance, but if a president failed to support his planners, could they cut off funds to force greater use of planning machinery or would the country's compelling development needs force the continuation of assistance despite the unfortunate fate of its planners?

During the development decade presidents, planners, and foreign technicians struggled over the integration of planning into national policy-making processes. The five cases that follow tell the story of their confrontations on the field of political battle.

Guatemala

Since its creation in 1954, the Guatemalan planning agency has suffered from presidential neglect. Initially it was a semi-autonomous agency created to advise the president, but it enjoyed little access to presidential policy-making. The planning agency was responsible to the Planning Council, which was composed of six cabinet ministers and two public bank directors. The ministers, who represented different parties and factions under President Ydígoras between 1958 and 1963, were too preoccupied with political conflict to pay attention to the planning agency. As the political struggle intensified in succeeding years, the planning agency fell into complete political isolation.

Despite the political irrelevancy of the planning agency, public investments were made in the name of development plans throughout the late 1950s. In the mid-1950s Castillo Armas, with the assistance of American technicians, made his development plan a conspicuous symbol of his public policies in order to identify himself with the development ideology made popular by the reformist Arevalo and Arbenz regimes that preceded him. Ydígoras, aware both of this ideology when he was inaugurated in 1958 and of the availability of American financial support for a noncommunist development policy, sought to enhance his own position by creating his "Ydígoras Plan." Under the plan, the Guatemalan government achieved 64 percent of its public investment goals between 1960 and 1964.[14]

Many of the development projects started by Ydígoras were continued by Colonel Peralta Azurdia, who overthrew him in March 1963. Peralta, who viewed himself as a temporary government caretaker, was reluctant to initiate new development policies, but he could not escape foreign and regional pressures to continue the activities of Guatemala's planning agency. Guatemala's neighbors were busy preparing Five Year Plans with the assistance of JOPLAN technicians, so Guatemala joined the procession. In late 1964 the Guatemalan government formally announced its plan for the 1965–69 period. In 1965, the plan's only full year under the Peralta administration, only 50 percent of its public investment objectives were reached.[15]

The Guatemalan planners blamed insufficient budgetary support for their shortcoming in 1965. Although legislative allocations had been sufficient, actual disbursement was inadequate because the government sold only 61 percent of the bonds needed to finance its development investments. Moreover, the planners

14. República de Guatemala, Consejo Nacional de Planificación Económica, *La planificación en Guatemala: su historia, problemas, y perspectivas* (Guatemala, 1969), p. 7.

15. Ibid., p. 64.

argued, numerous government agencies had not prepared themselves to manage new programs and, consequently, they failed to use even those funds that were disbursed to them.[16]

Guatemala's planning process must also bear some of the responsibility for the public investment failures in 1965. The president had encouraged the designing of a plan in order to conform with his neighbors and with foreign demands, but he had no interest in plan coordination and implementation. To the planners' displeasure, the budget office of the Finance Ministry continued to guard its powers of budget management and refused to share expenditure data with the planning agency. Only by working around the budget office could the planners supervise ministerial management of development projects. Not long after the official presentation of the Five Year Plan in 1964, the planning agency became, in effect, an organization in search of a function, for as a CIAP report points out, "during the early part of 1966 the internal activities of the planning agency lost their momentum. ... The necessary steps were not taken to consolidate an effective national planning system by setting up and operating the sectoral regional units. Nor were any general specific policy measures adopted with regard to implementation of the national plan, so that whether or not it was carried out depended purely on the dynamism of the system."[17]

Peralta's three-and-one-half year rule represented a holding action. He had taken power without a coherent development program and his single concern remained the imposition of order on the conflict-ridden Guatemalan political process. Like a stern father, he attempted to put his family finances in order. His development investments reflected this perspective. He initiated little but continued that which had preceded him. He purged the public administration of a few of its corrupt officials, but made no effort to shape that administration to manage de-

16. República de Guatemala, Ministerio de Hacienda y Crédito Público, Dirección Técnica del Presupuesto, *Control y medición de resultados del presupuesto por programas del año 1965* (Guatemala, 1966).
17. OAS Secretariat, *Domestic Efforts and the Needs for External Financing for the Development of Guatemala* (Washington, 1966), p. 26.

velopment policies more efficiently. Guerilla warfare and political terrorism continued between the left and right, but no political equilibrium was created; only the budget was balanced.

Plan performance declined under elected President Méndez Montenegro as only 41, 39, and 34 percent of public investment objectives were fulfilled in 1966, 1967, and 1968, respectively.[18] Nor did the planning process improve under Méndez. Although concerned with the expansion of public investment, Méndez was forced to direct his attention to questions of political survival rather than administrative coordination. The Planning Council met only sporadically and became a minor forum for the expression of independent complaints of ministers rather than a means to formulate and manage development policy. By 1969 a CIAP team concluded after its annual review of Guatemalan planning that the Planning Council's "role had decreased in recent years, particularly in 1967 and 1968. It has no decision-making power and has been reduced to a forum for inter-ministerial consultation on particular projects over whose execution the Planning Council actually exercised little control."[19]

Guatemalan presidents have been too preoccupied with political conflict to bother with planning. Planning, though designed to impose order on governmental decision-making, at the same time requires a relatively stable political process in which to operate. No such environment existed in Guatemala. On the contrary, presidents have been obsessed with holding power through their mediation of intense political conflict and have given little attention to the imposition of order on their policy-making processes. Survival, not control, has been their objective. Under these conditions the planners' functions have been reduced to communicating with international agencies and creating the documents required for foreign assistance.

Although Guatemalans desire political stability, few can agree on the purpose and form of that stability. Each faction fears that

18. República de Guatemala, Consejo Nacional de Planificación Económica, *La planificatión en Guatemala.*

19. OEA Secretaria, *El esfuerzo interno y las necesidades de financiamiento externo para el desarrollo de Guatemala* (Washington, 1969), pp. 73–74.

the success of another will mean the obstruction of the attainment of its own goals. As a result, obstruction of others has become the means of preventing one's own destruction. One of the principal players in the Guatemalan political game during the development decade spoke for his frustrated colleagues when he summed up their despair by concluding: "We are confronted by a situation in which political conditions impede the adoption of policies that we recognize are necessary to create political stability. One could conclude that we are trapped by a form of vicious circle: it is impossible to promulgate policies that assure political stability because there is not political stability; and by not making these policies, we cannot hope to achieve political stability."[20]

Nicaragua

Like the Guatemalans, the Nicaraguans created their first planning agency under IBRD tutelage in the early 1950s. But the Nicaraguan agency fell into neglect and disuse soon thereafter. Not until its leaders acknowledged the new demands of the Alliance for Progress in 1961 did official attention again return to the planning agency. As with many other requirements of the Alliance, development planning was enthusiastically embraced by Nicaraguan officials upon their return from the Punta del Este meeting. Their support of planning, however, proved more symbolic than substantive, for, as the young planners tried to redesign Nicaragua's development programs, they encountered increasing opposition from the entrenched officials who suddenly viewed them as rivals for President Luis Somoza's support. To this opposition was eventually added the distrust of Anastasio Somoza Debayle, elected president in 1967, whose personalistic style clashed with the planners' policy-making innovations. Consequently, by 1969 the planning agency had fallen into almost complete neglect.

20. OEA, *Informe final del subcomité del CIAP sobre Guatemala* (Washington, 1968), p. 15. The statement was made by economist Alberto Fuentes Mohr, who was removed from his position of Finance Minister during a tax reform crisis in early 1968. After serving a year at the Central American Bank he returned to Guatemala as Foreign Minister in 1969.

The creation of planning machinery in Nicaragua was largely a one-man effort. Antioco Sacasa Sarria, an American-trained economist, submitted a proposal to Luis Somoza in late 1961 calling for a planning agency with direct ties to the president and full responsibility for long-range planning for the public and private sectors. As the enthusiasm of the cabinet ministers became tempered by their increasing perception of the potential policy-making power of the planning agency, they united in opposition to Sacasa's proposal. President Luis Somoza, however, was closely attuned to the demands of international agencies and accepted the proposal over ministerial objections. To placate the ministers, he reinstituted the old National Economic Council to act in an advisory capacity, paralleling, but not controlling the planning agency.[21]

The new planning agency began with a talent shortage, for the IBRD mission that had created a planning agency in the mid-1950s had failed to train technicians to staff it. To remedy his personnel problem Sacasa drafted his economics students at the National University who, with the assistance of the regional Joint Planning Mission, designed Nicaragua's first Five Year Plan. The planners, however, had little opportunity to influence the policies of Luis Somoza for he left office in May 1963, before their plan was completed. It was not until after the inauguration of his successor, long-time Somoza colleague René Schick, that the planners began to assert their demands on the Nicaraguan president.

The Nicaraguan planners proudly fulfilled 75 and 78 percent of their public investment goals in 1965 and 1966, respectively.[22] But these accomplishments are deceptive, for under Schick the planning agency descended from its formal ties to the presidency to complete isolation from presidential decision-making. As long

21. República de Nicaragua, Decreto Ejecutivo Num. 52, 31 de enero de 1962. The National Economic Council included the Ministers of Economy, Treasury, Development, and Agriculture as well as the Directors of the National Bank, the Central Bank, and the Development Institute.

22. República de Nicaragua, Consejo Nacional de Economiá, Oficina de Planificación, *El desarrollo económico y social de Nicaragua* (Managua, 1967), Cuadros XII–5 and XIII–9.

as Luis Somoza had been formally committed to planning, the planning agency continued tied in form if not in fact to the president's office. But René Schick had made no such commitment. To a greater extent than his predecessor, Schick relied on his cabinet members for advice, seeking to balance their wants in order to gain their personal approval. One measure that all of the ministers agreed on was the removal of the planning agency from its direct ties to the president. Leading the ministerial challenge was Francisco Lainez, the Central Bank director, who, as the economic czar who had designed the conservative fiscal and monetary policies promulgated by the Somozas, resented Sacasa's proposals for expanded public expenditures, especially in social infrastructure, and for greater export diversification. Working through the less-domineering Schick, Lainez eliminated Sacasa's threat when the legislature enacted a reorganization proposal that made the planning agency an advisory group to the National Economic Council. Under the disinterested ministerial Council, the planners lost most of their power to coordinate and control policy implementation.[23]

Despite its demotion, the planning agency produced a Five Year Plan in 1964. Nevertheless, it was soon clear to outside observers that the Nicaraguan president had sacrificed his planning agency to the ministerial wolves. In 1967 a CIAP team concluded that: "Until the present time there has not been an integral program encompassing real variables and the integration of internal resources for guiding the economic and social policy in the nation. In addition, there does not exist an adequate relationship between the planning agency and the various central government and autonomous agencies that execute programs. Equally, there is a lack of a central planning office tied directly to the president where it can aid in the elaboration, control and coordination of programs."[24]

The planning agency's decline was completed after the inauguration of General Anastasio Somoza Debayle, the younger

23. Ibid., pp. II–9—II–12.
24. OEA Secretaria, *El esfuerzo interno y las necesidades de financiamiento externo para el desarrollo de Nicaragua* (Washington, 1968), p. 82.

of the Somoza brothers, in May 1967. What was disappearing under Schick, virtually ceased to operate under Somoza. He buried the planning agency within his ministerial structure by relocating it within the Ministry of Economy where its only function became the collection of economic data. In exasperation, Antioco Sacasa resigned from the agency soon thereafter. Ironically, a major economic and financial crisis engulfed Nicaragua immediately after Sacasa departed. The crisis was caused in large part by three successive years of drought which badly damaged the cotton crop and with it Nicaragua's national productivity. The intensity of the crisis in 1968 was due, in large part, to the failure of Nicaraguan policy-makers to react to the first and second droughts in 1965 and 1966. Later some even argued that this would not have been the case if Somoza had made use of his planners and their analysis during those two years.[25] But instead of rationally examining policy alternatives as the problems arose, he waited until he was engulfed by economic crisis and then reacted by imposing his own drastic stabilization program.

Economic planning did not fit well into the Nicaraguan policy-making process. One might have hoped, as did the first Nicaraguan planners, that planning would prosper in a system dominated by a strong presidency and centrally controlled decision-making. But while these conditions may be necessary, they are not sufficient for effective planning. The Somozas' style of rule was very personalistic and unsystematic. The planners threatened this style and the administrative elite which has survived within it. As a result, instead of forcing greater use of planning, the economic crisis of 1968 only stimulated a new assertion of the Somozas' personalistic control.

Honduras

Honduras also initiated planning under the guidance of the IBRD in the mid-1950s. However, as in Nicaragua, the planning agency remained a very marginal participant in Honduran policy-making after its creation. Not until the last two years of the

25. CIAP technicians made this point in OEA Secretaria, *El esfuerzo interno y las necesidades de financiamiento externo para el desarrollo de Nicaragua* (Washington, 1969), p. 8.

administration of President Villeda Morales did it try to design a public investment program. Villeda, anxious to use the opportunities offered by the Alliance for Progress in 1961, instructed his planning agency to prepare development projects for Alliance financing. As a result, Honduras became the seventh Latin American country to submit a national development program to Alliance administrators in 1962.[26]

Despite Villeda's revitalization of his Planning Council, the CIAP committee that evaluated Honduras' 1963–64 development plan warned that Honduras' planning machinery was wholly unequipped to coordinate plan implementation.[27] Nevertheless, not until 1965 did the Honduran government respond to external pressures to reorganize its planning operations. In that year the formerly semi-autonomous planning agency was attached to the office of the president, it was given budgetary review powers, and it was authorized to inspect the development projects of all ministries and autonomous agencies.[28]

The 1965–69 Five Year Plan designed by the planning agency, like those of its neighbors, was far more ambitious than past public investment programs. It reflected the naive optimism of Honduran planners and their JOPLAN advisors, who believed that they could plunge simultaneously into a wide variety of development projects. But instead, they managed to fulfill only 54, 36, and 41 percent of their public investment goals in 1965, 1966, and 1967, respectively.[29] Numerous explanations for these disappointing performances have been offered. The Honduran planners estimated that "approximately 16 percent of the reason

26. Economist Intelligence Unit, *Three Monthly Economic Review— Central America*, no. 35 (October 1961), p. 16; no. 37 (April 1962), p. 13.

27. OAS Secretariat, *Domestic Efforts and the Needs for External Financing for the Development of Honduras* (Washington, 1966), p. 72.

28. República de Honduras, Ley Num. 30, octubre de 1965. The membership of the council remained the same under the new law, but it established, in theory at least, stronger ties between the executive secretary of the planning agency and the president.

29. República de Honduras, Consejo Superior de Planificación Económica, *Inversiones realizadas durante 1965, 1966, y 1967* (Tegucigalpa, 1968).

is a lack of financing; 41 percent, slowness in procedures for obtaining foreign loans, a slowness that, naturally may be our fault or the fault of the international agencies; 20 percent, operational defects, that is to say, the inability of our agencies to carry out operations; and the remaining 23 percent, other causes."[30] The specific operational defects noted by the planners included: the absence of project studies and implementation calendars, the indecisiveness of public officials, unqualified personnel, the use of money for purposes other than those programmed, and antiquated procurement procedures.[31] Unfortunately, the planners suggested few remedies for these problems. In fact, in their analyses of plan performance in 1966 and 1967 they simply listed exactly the same obstacles they had identified in 1965 but again omitted suggestions about the means for their elimination.[32]

International agencies were particularly frustrated by the Honduran failure to disburse loans rapidly and, in their evaluations, urged the elimination of some specific roadblocks. They pointed primarily at the planning agency and the Public Works Ministry as the major bottlenecks. The planning agency, they argued, exercised insufficient control over program implementation. The Public Works Ministry, they added, was not structured, staffed, and equipped to manage its rapidly expanding volume of projects.[33]

Frustrated by what he considered unjust foreign criticism and inadequate presidential support, Miguel Angel Rivera, the executive secretary of the planning agency, in July 1967 unexpectedly resigned in protest. As executive secretary, Rivera had been responsible for prodding the ministers into implementation of the Five Year Plan. But he failed to gain their cooperation. His failure, he argued, was caused not by a lack of effort on his part, but by the reluctance of President López to support him.

30. OAS, *Final Report of the CIAP Subcommittee on Honduras* (Washington, 1965), p. 17.

31. República de Honduras, Consejo Superior de Planificación Económica, *Inversiones Realizadas . . . 1967*.

32. Ibid.

33. OAS Secretariat, *Domestic Efforts and the Needs for External Financing for Development in Honduras*, pp. 53–55.

More specifically, he blamed the isolation of the president which was managed by his chief political aide and personal secretary, Ricardo Zuñiga, an aggressive and ambitious Nationalist party leader.

The politically inexperienced Colonel López had appointed Zuñiga as his personal secretary in order to secure Nationalist party support after he overthrew Villeda in the fall of 1963. Since then Zuñiga, in asserting his own influence over national policy-making, had sheltered the less aggressive López from the influence of technicians like Rivera who sought greater policy-making authority. Frustrated by Zuñiga's interference, Rivera finally protested publicly that:

The Secretary to the Presidency has become a one man office that refuses to delegate responsibility and authority; this has made it a point of strangulation for information directed to the President and has destroyed its utility as a strong agent in development policy-making. At the beginning of the present administration, the only function of this office was political patronage, most of which has been very detrimental to the operation of the public administration. . . . On the other hand, there has not been developed, as was promised by the President's Secretary, the Group of Three, composed of the President's Secretary, the Minister of Economy and Finance and the Executive Secretary of the Planning Council, whose task it was to investigate the causes of delays in the implementation of various projects.[34]

In early July 1967, Rivera offered President López a choice: either remove Ricardo Zuñiga or accept Rivera's resignation. López quickly decided that his technician was more expendable than was his chief political advisor.

Economic planners fought and temporarily lost their battle for influence in the Honduran government. Initiated in the early 1950s, planning was isolated from policy-making until it was attached to the presidency in response to demands of Alliance for Progress administrators. Although international agencies have persistently demanded the use of planning by Honduran policy-makers, the planners were isolated from presidential power by

34. Quoted in the Tegucigalpa daily newspaper, *El Pueblo*, 12 July 1967.

the jealous political associates of President López who prospered through their personal manipulation of the bureaucracy and viewed the planners as rivals for political power.

Development policy execution is a very new activity in Honduras. Dominated by parochialism and the regional dispersion of political power, Hondurans have never demanded an active, well-guided central administration. In fact, the Honduran art of presidential rule is still dominated by the disbursement of small favors rather than the delivery of large development projects. Although under intense pressure from some of their own technicians and international agencies to reverse this tradition, Honduran presidents have followed the development path very cautiously, for their political survival still requires their careful management of the cooperation of numerous provincial interests. The rise to power of the military has not significantly altered this process, for the military, reflecting Honduran society, is also dominated by particularistic interests and regional power centers. The challenge of development policy-making, then, is a challenge to the entire Honduran political system, for centrally coordinated policy-making requires a concentration of governmental power that threatens the traditional political process.

The reluctant Honduran president faces overwhelming external pressure to accelerate his consolidation of political and administrative power and apply it to development policy-making. Through no choice of their own, the Hondurans have become an important link in Central America's regional integration and Honduran backwardness is a serious obstacle to the region's balanced economic growth. Regional and international agencies, although frustrated with Honduras' past performance, continued to insist that it rapidly expand its development programs through the use of abundant foreign financial support. Yet, despite all of these demands facing the Honduran president, he submerged his planners under the constraints of personalism, political rivalry, and administrative intransigence.

El Salvador

After the Punta del Este meeting the military-civilian junta that had taken power in January 1961 decided that the political salvation of their government and the economic development of their country lay with the Alliance for Progress. One of their first acts to demonstrate their acceptance of the Alliance was the creation of a National Planning Council (CONAPLAN) and a planning agency in April 1962. The Council included the Salvadorian president as chairman, all cabinet ministers, the Central Bank director, and representatives of the private sector.[35]

The new planning agency quickly fell under North American influence. Its initial operations were supported primarily by an American loan and a team of consultants from the firm of Robert R. Nathan assisted in the organization of the agency and the designing of development plans during the rest of the decade. El Salvador's 1965–69 Five Year Plan was written primarily by the Robert Nathan consultants and the JOPLAN mission.

Largely because of financial problems, the Salvadorians fulfilled only 49 and 24 percent of their public investment goals in 1966 and 1967, respectively, after having reached 75 percent in 1965.[36] The planners also blamed several administrative obstacles for their performance decline, for they discovered a lack of program control in several ministries and the absence of coordination between the planning agency and the implementing agencies.[37] By 1967 President Sánchez was forced to respond to foreign pressures to improve plan performance by accepting Inter-American Bank assistance with project preparation. The basic pattern of agency operations remained unchanged, however. Sánchez did very little because he was handicapped by political and administrative constraints which, in the policy conflicts between his planners and ministers, forced him to support his ministers whose backing he needed to maintain control over his coalition National Conciliation party.

The administrative independence of governmental agencies also obstructed the planners' control over program implemen-

---

35. República de El Salvador, Decreto Num. 59, abril de 1962.

36. Unpublished data supplied by El Salvador's Consejo Nacional de Planificación y Coordinación Económica.

37. República de El Salvador, Consejo Nacional de Planificación y Coordinación Económica, *Informe trimestral de inversión pública al diciembre de 1966* (San Salvador, 1967), pp. i–iii.

tation. Tasks as deceptively simple as the collection of project information often eluded the planners because of ministerial refusal to collect and communicate such information. Agency personnel saw themselves as responsible only to the agency directors who, in turn, viewed themselves responsible only to the personal commands of the president. Consequently, the formal sanction of presidential authority was not sufficient to legitimize the planners' demands for cooperation; only the personal command of the president could do so, and, as we have seen, Salvadorian presidents were reluctant to give those commands.

Planning was a new policy-making instrument that accompanied El Salvador's acceptance of the Alliance for Progress. Its operations were dominated by skilled American technicians, but its impact on policy-making has been minimal. It was neither ignored nor suppressed by Salvadorian presidents, but was forced to compete openly with other political forces for presidential support. In these open political battles its meager political resources were insufficient to gain the support and authority it required.

Costa Rica

Despite the expansion of development and welfare programs by President José Figueres and his National Liberation party in the mid-1950s, Costa Rica was the last Central American country to create a planning agency. After the PLN returned to the presidency in 1962, serious consideration was given to the creation of a planning agency, but President Orlich, like other Central American presidents before him, was reluctant to invite the publicity and scrutiny of his policies that would surely follow annual reports on the quantitative successes and failures of a national plan. Nevertheless, under pressure to fulfill Costa Rica's obligations under the charter of the Alliance for Progress, the Costa Rican government created a planning agency (OFIPLAN) in early 1963 composed of seven departments and attached to the office of the president.[38]

38. República de Costa Rica, Ley de Planificación, Num. 3087, 31 de enero de 1963. The structure of OFIPLAN was similar to that of the region's other planning agencies. It included departments of: 1) admini-

OFIPLAN dutifully created the Costa Rican 1965–69 Five Year Plan in late 1964. The plan, however, was as much a challenge as a solution to Orlich's policy-making problems. It required large public investments at a time when Costa Rica was experiencing a grave fiscal crisis and it asked the president to coordinate the activities of 51 autonomous agencies that had traditionally guarded their independence.

The Costa Ricans managed to fulfill 64 and 56 percent of their public investment goals in 1965 and 1966, respectively.[39] It is apparent, however, that Orlich did not fully understand his planners nor did the confusion that surrounded their initial efforts inspire his trust. The planners now admit that their Five Year Plan was based on insufficient and inaccurate data and claim that they were rushed into preparing a plan because it was demanded as a condition of foreign assistance.[40] They also blamed Costa Rica's traditional budgetary process, its decentralized administrative structure, and the unwillingness of the president to support them. Even though the budget office is part of OFIPLAN, its behavior is restricted by the National Finance Law that assigns strong disbursement controls to the Treasury, which is guided in its allocations by the requirement that its monthly disbursements to all agencies be balanced with incoming revenues. Such a rigid system offers no flexibility to meet the fluctuating financial demands of various government programs.

The national administrative structure enhances resistance by the ministries and the autonomous agencies to increased coordi-

---

strative efficiency; 2) long-range and medium-range plans; 3) annual plans; 4) project evaluation; 5) program control; and 6) finance. Its staff increased from 37 in 1963 to 69 in 1968 and its operating costs rose from $180,000 to $220,000 during the same period.

39. República de Costa Rica, Presidencia de la República, Oficina de Planificación, *Observaciones a la ejecución del plan nacional de desarrollo 1965–1968* (San José, 1968).

40. While never made public, these initial difficulties were discussed in an unpublished paper written by four OFIPLAN officials for presentation at the University of Costa Rica, see Luis Edwin Vargas Sanabria, Luis Fernando Chaves Solera, Miguel Masis Acosta, y Alvaro Hernandez Rodriquez, "La planificación en Costa Rica" (thesis, Universidad Nacional de Costa Rica, 1968), p. 11.

nation of their public investments. Surprisingly, OFIPLAN does not have automatic access to agency information but must receive special authorization from each agency to review its investment plans. Agencies, fearing loss of autonomy, often ignored OFIPLAN inquiries. Consequently, Costa Rican planners frequently complained that Article 188 of the 1949 Constitution which grants autonomy to executive agencies has caused:

each of the autonomous institutes to believe that its functions are the most important in the government. They have been preoccupied with accomplishing their own objectives without concern for other agencies, and they have considered their function as an end and not a means for national economic and social progress. . . . The excessive independence enjoyed by these institutions creates problems and maladjustments in public administration, many of which originate in the failure to coordinate agency expenditures with the policies of the Central Government and the economic situation of the country.[41]

Orlich was aware of the legal and political constraints on OFIPLAN's operations, but he applied little pressure to remove them. He preferred the traditional allocative process of using the public treasury to satisfy the different claims of his ministries and agencies. To this he added the use of foreign loans to satisfy agency claims. Ironically, he made policy in a time of financial crisis, yet rather than use planning as a technique for establishing priorities to guide his use of scarce resources, he placed his trust in his political intuition.

The PLN lost the presidency in 1966 when José Trejos, a conservative economist, was elected president with the support of a coalition of anti-PLN conservative parties. Trejos opposed economic planning in principle and had little confidence in the PLN-appointed technicians who staffed his planning agency. He appointed as OFIPLAN director a man with no planning training or experience who had continually criticized OFIPLAN's work as "planning by aloof economists who were far removed from concrete realities."[42] Trejos was soon embarassed by his incom-

41. Ibid., p. 12.
42. OEA, *Informe final del subcomité del CIAP sobre Costa Rica* (Washington, 1967), p. 13.

petent director and replaced him in the fall of 1968 with a young economist trained at the University of California. Under Trejos OFIPLAN concentrated on controlling and reducing government expenditures. In the process they fulfilled only 50 and 43 percent of their public investment goals in 1967 and 1968, respectively.[43] It was apparent that Trejos had reduced OFIPLAN to little more than an enlarged budget office by the time he left office in 1970. As a CIAP report concluded, under Trejos OFIPLAN underwent "a regression in some aspects."[44]

Since 1963 planning has formed a small part of the Costa Rican policy-making process. Created primarily in response to the demands of the Alliance for Progress, its operations were restricted by the forces of administrative tradition, ideology, and political expediency. While Costa Rican presidents recognized the symbolic importance of planning in their negotiations with international agencies, they continued to allocate their financial resources primarily through traditional bargaining with powerholders in their ministries and agencies.

THE FATE OF PLANNING

The synoptic model of planning was not attained in Central America during the development decade; in fact, it was not even approximated in any of the five countries. Everywhere planners adjusted to traditional policy-making conditions and patterns, rather than vice versa. To be sure, plans were designed and development policies were promulgated, but such efforts resulted as much from the traditional process of public investment decision-making as from the reshaping of policy-making by means of the application of synoptic techniques.

Lindblom's recognition of the cognitive impossibility of the synoptic model is, in part, appropriate to Central America. In 1964 the planners had little time and even less data upon which to create their Five Year Plans. And even with abundant foreign

43. República de Costa Rica, Presidencia de la República, Oficina de Planificación, *Observaciones . . . 1965–1968.*

44. OAS Secretariat, *Domestic Efforts and the Need for External Financing for the Development of Costa Rica* (Washington, 1967), p. 6.

advice they could not fully examine more than a handful of policy instruments and objectives.

The planners' major problem, however, was not cognitive, but political. Planning is an orderly process; traditional mediation of political conflict is not. In attempting to coordinate development policy-making through the explicit definition of objectives and the selection of policy instruments, the planners were demanding a basic change in the traditional means of competitively selecting policy alternatives. In doing so, they threatened not only the power contenders who had enriched themselves through the traditional process but also the bargaining flexibility required by presidents to mediate policy conflict and enhance their own political power.

The planners discovered that when Central American presidents had committed themselves to new development policies, they had not committed themselves to new policy-making processes. Presidents had assumed that, with the addition of a few new public institutions, they could expand development policies without substantially altering their decision-making procedures. Planning agencies, created largely at the insistence of international and regional agencies, were originally tolerated by Central American presidents as just another of their many new development-oriented agencies. But as the planners began to intervene not simply as representatives of another bargaining agency but as aspiring framers of presidential policy decisions, the presidents, themselves accustomed to very little staff assistance, vigorously resisted the planners' encroachments on their prerogatives. Thus, the presidents' dilemma of integrating planning without threatening other power contenders was easily resolved in favor of the power contenders and against the planners. Equally apparent was the resolution of the planners' dilemma of forcing change without losing presidential support as they increasingly lost the support they so desperately sought.

The process of partisan mutual adjustment identified by Lindblom and Gross as the likely alternative to the imposition of synoptic decision-making describes a system of open bargaining in which the winners and losers are constantly changing. While this may be an accurate description of some policy-making systems, it is not entirely appropriate to the experience of planning in Central America, for it assumes that the planners shared influence with other power contenders and could effectively bargain with them. In fact, the planners enjoyed no such power. The young technicians had few personal ties with their presidents and their importance to presidential success was more symbolic than substantive; they were primarily tools manipulated to secure the financial support of international agencies. Thus, partisan adjustment in the Central American policy-making systems was not mutual as described by Lindblom and Gross, but one-sided and weighted against the planners.[45]

The five national planning experiences yield some insight into the principal obstacles to planning in developing countries. Recognition of these obstacles also suggests some of the conditions that might be necessary for more effective planning operations. It is clear that planning is ineffective in a system like that of Guatemala which is dominated by persistent political instability resulting from fundamental disagreement over the rules of the national political game. To presidents coping with such open political warfare planning simply appears irrelevant. Guatemala points to the need for some political order within which planning can operate. Order is, however, a necessary but not a sufficient condition for effective planning. Honduras, for example, enjoyed political order under López after 1963. But López lacked another necessary condition—effective presidential control needed to enforce the plan's directives. Because of his insecurity and dependence on self-serving party leaders, he was unable to enforce his own development program.

Moving a step further, we see that even if political stability is combined with presidential political control, planning may still flounder. Both conditions prevailed in Nicaragua where planning suffered a dismal fate at the hands of the well-entrenched Somozas. In Nicaragua planning was obstructed by the Somozas' anxious exercise of presidential power and their defensive reaction to the ambitious *técnicos*. Thus, where presidential con-

45. The planners self-perception of failure, which was revealed in interviews, is supported by the CIAP reports; see Note on Sources.

trol is dependent on the erratic use of personal force, planning again tends to flounder. Yet, as in Costa Rica and El Salvador where the presidency is more institutionalized, other obstacles had to be confronted: jealous Central Banks, ambitious autonomous agencies, and patronage-ridden ministries persistently resisted the planners' demands.

In sum, there are a handful of conditions which we might consider necessary for effective development planning. Political order is an obvious prerequisite; some centralized presidential power is also useful, particularly when based on legitimate rules and norms rather than personal will and force. To this list must be added the cooperation, or at least the tolerance, of government agencies.

But the fact remains, in the real world of development policymaking most of these conditions do not exist. Nevertheless, development policy decisions are continually made and, with varying degrees of success, implemented. Of interest then is not how these favorable conditions can be created, but how policy is made in their absence. Once again we turn to the Central American experience for an answer, this time by examining the mobilization and allocation of development resources under adverse conditions.

4

Taxing and Spending
for Development

The Central American planners were very ambitious young men. They set particularly high goals for themselves and their governments when they created their Five Year Plans for the 1965–69 period. For example, they proposed the expansion of public investment from the $123 million they spent in 1964 to $315 million in 1969, an increase of 156 percent in five years.[1] They recognized that the price for this expansion was high but they managed to convince themselves that they could extract sufficient funds from both international and national sources to cover their increasing investments. In the Alliance for Progress they, and their political superiors, saw the opportunity for low-interest loans to pay the foreign exchange costs of the projects included in their plans; they were equally confident that they could match these loans with national funding by increasing public revenues. Moreover, they were particularly encouraged by the fact that when they designed their plans in 1964 the region had substantially recovered from the adverse effects of its post-1958 recession and the five economies were once again expanding at high rates.[2]

1. SIECA, Mision Conjunta de Programación, *Resumen de los planes centroamericanos de desarrollo económico y social para el periódo 1965–1969* (Guatemala, 1965). p. 41.
2. The national and regional planners interviewed readily admitted

The planners' task of revenue generation confronted both old and new obstacles. Among the former were their traditional tax structures. As we saw, the Central American presidents tampered with their tax structures in the early 1950s, but left them essentially intact. Consequently, the planners inherited tax structures that were tied largely to foreign trade and were vulnerable to its vicissitudes. Not only were these structures vulnerable, but they also failed to extract very large amounts of resources from the Central American economies. For example, in 1961 total central government tax revenue throughout the region averaged only 8.6 percent of regional gross national product.[3] Equally significant, per capita central government income averaged only $26.11 in the region. Most distressing, however, was the fact that in this region of approximately 13 million people, only 48,677 individuals and firms paid income taxes in 1961.[4] Central America's continued dependence on indirect taxation, particularly import tariffs, is clearly revealed in Table 3.

TABLE 3
Import and Income Taxes as a Percentage of Government Revenue, 1960

	Import	Income	Other
Costa Rica	54.5	10.7	34.8
El Salvador	40.8	8.0	51.2
Guatemala	31.8	7.3	59.9
Honduras	48.3	14.9	36.8
Nicaragua	45.5	9.8	44.7
Central America	44.2	10.1	45.7

Source: ESAPAC, *Estudio comparativo de sistemas tributarios de los países centroamericanos* (San José, 1966), pp. 16, 27.

The newest revenue policy obstacle encountered by the planners was a product not of the tax structures as they existed in 1960 but of adverse changes in them caused by the Common

their naive optimism in 1964 when they initiated their first Five Year Plans; see Note on Sources.

3. ESAPAC, *Estudio comparativo de sistemas tributarios de los paises centroamericanos* (San José, 1966), p. 9.

4. Ibid., p. 19.

Market tariff agreements after 1960. Predictably, the creation of free trade within the Common Market led to a significant decline in import duties as a percent of total revenue; by 1966, in fact, import duties composed only 35 percent of central government revenue, a drop of 8.4 percent from 1961.[5] More important, import duties as a percent of import value also dropped significantly. (See Table 4.)

TABLE 4
Import Duties as a Percent of Import Value

	1960	1966
Costa Rica	22	19
El Salvador	20	10
Guatemala	18	11
Honduras	22	9
Nicaragua	20	10
Central America	*20*	*12*

Source: Computed from OEA, *El avance de la integración centroamericana y las necesidades de financiamiento externo* (Washington, 1968), Anexo A, pp. 31–37, 40.

The success of the planners depended, in large part, on their ability to compensate for these imposing fiscal obstacles through the selection and management of innovative revenue policy instruments, and it was to this task that they turned much of their attention after completing their Five Year Plans in 1964. In their attempts to influence revenue policy-making they were not alone, but found themselves part of shifting alliances that varied from issue to issue and policy instrument to policy instrument. In the presidents who faced popular and foreign pressure to complete their development project commitments they found an occasional ally; but these same presidents, under counter pressure from political forces that opposed revenue policy innovation, often were forced to abandon their planners' cause. In the international agencies who financed their projects they also found support for

5. Computed from OEA, *El avance de la integración centroamericana y las necesidades de financiamiento externo* (Washington, 1968), Annexo C, p. 40.

their revenue policy proposals, but the international agencies too proved to be unreliable allies.

Most striking about the revenue policy instruments used by the Central American governments during the development decade was their variety. Constant frustration with fiscal policy problems produced a continual search for new policy initiatives. Almost frantically, the five governments experimented with tax reform, austerity budgets, the manipulation of foreign assistance, and the regional coordination of fiscal policy in seeking to mobilize resources to support their development plans. Equally striking was the inadequacy of all of these instruments in meeting each government's total development resource needs. Instead of discovering a general solution, they managed only to make successive adjustments that succeeded in supporting a minimum of their policy objectives. Much of the story of the planners' impact on policy-making lies in their revenue policy struggles, for the use of each new instrument confronted them with the obstacles that limited their success throughout the decade.

TAX REFORM

Since World War II tax reform has been a major policy objective of reform governments throughout Latin America. Many have considered it necessary not only to finance development programs but also to more equitably distribute income for purposes of social justice and economic growth. Equally important, however, has been the widespread opposition to tax reform throughout the hemisphere. Landed elites have obstructed the enforcement of land taxes where they could not prevent their enactment; commercial farmers have successfully threatened their withdrawal from production as a means of obstructing tax reform; industrial firms have often received tax incentives rather than tax burdens in exchange for their willingness to invest and produce; and most members of the salaried middle class have fought against more progressive income taxes, for they know that they alone cannot avoid their payment. In Central America, where governments are often dependent on the cooperation of a wealthy minority of their citizenry for the successful performance of their economies, all of these forces have obstructed tax reform. In the 1950s, as we have seen, the only significant new taxes to succeed were those directed at the foreign-owned banana companies. All other reforms were minor incremental changes in existing, particularly import, taxes.

The planners were quick to apply the fiscal policy lessons they had learned at ECLA. Foremost among these was the restructuring of the region's antiquated tax structures. To support their case for tax reform they drew upon the orthodox development strategy that had been partially applied in the 1950s and the neo-orthodox doctrine of the early 1960s, both of which had urged tax reform. Moreover, the Alliance for Progress agreement also required tax reform. Thus, after the historic meeting at Punta del Este, Central American presidents found themselves faced by an unpopular yet unavoidable demand for revenue policy innovation. To have ignored it would have meant their loss of much needed foreign financial assistance. But to enact and implement it they would have to overcome or circumvent the traditional threats of elite and middle class opposition. Confronted by these contrasting demands, each president worked out his own strategy for coping with his revenue policy dilemma.

Presidents Villeda of Honduras and Ydígoras of Guatemala strongly desired Alliance assistance in 1962, yet both realized that they would have to enact unpopular tax reforms in order to receive it. Villeda already faced strong internal opposition from Honduras' Nationalist party, which vigorously opposed his reform initiatives and his attempt to build a personal power base; simultaneously, the Honduran Army was becoming very anxious over his creation of a Civilian Guard to counter their influence in the countryside. Villeda nevertheless insisted that his Liberal party-controlled Congress enact major tax reform legislation early in 1963. But once enacted, the reforms were never implemented, for their promulgation was cut short by a military coup that removed Villeda and rescinded his tax legislation in October 1963.

Similarly President Ydígoras faced intense opposition to tax reform in Guatemala from the oligarchy-dominated Association of Agriculturists, the Chamber of Commerce, and the Association of Industries. Predictably, his first tax reform bill was defeated by the opposition's majority in Congress in 1961—the eighth such tax bill to have been submitted unsuccessfully in ten years. Then, in the congressional elections of December 1961, Ydígoras' Redención party, amid shouts of fraud, increased its membership from 25 to 50 of 66 seats. Simultaneously, however, Guatemala's activist military, disillusioned by Ydígoras' inability to suppress his vocal, and sometimes violent, opposition, forced him to concede them most of his cabinet ministries. Thus, paradoxically, as Ydígoras captured most of the legislature, he lost much of his control over the executive.[6]

Trapped by fiscal necessities and political realities, Ydígoras chose to act on the former and used his new legislative majority to enact an income tax reform in November 1962. This was immediately followed by strong denunciations from Guatemala's agricultural and commercial associations, which took out full-page ads in local newspapers claiming that they would not pay the income tax or the emergency taxes on real estate, inheritance, and gasoline because of the government's "lack of capacity, sincerity, organization and guarantees of security."[7] But before the opposition's roar subsided, Ydígoras was removed by the military on March 1, 1963, amid cheers from all opposition parties.

The fate of tax reform in El Salvador was more complicated. In October 1960 President Lemus, a leader of the ruling PRUD party, was replaced by a leftist military-civilian junta which promised free elections, land reform, and tax reforms. The junta's rule was short-lived, however, for in January 1961 it was forcibly replaced by more conservative officers and civilians, who claimed they had acted to stop advancing communism which was about to "destroy democratic values and upset the economic structure."[8] To satisfy some of the reform demands unleashed by its predecessor, the new junta, led by Lieutenant Colonel Julio

6. Economist Intelligence Unit, *Three Monthly Review—Central America*, no. 38 (June 1962), p. 3; no. 39 (September 1962), p. 5.

7. *Hispanic American Report*, March 1963, p. 23.

8. Economist Intelligence Unit, *Three Monthly Review—Central America*, no. 33 (April 1961), p. 3.

Rivera, initiated an income tax reform raising rates by 50 percent among upper income groups and a new tax on reinvested profit.[9] As expected, the upper class landowners and businessmen protested the income tax increase. Soon thereafter the conservative Rivera junta, in an attempt to placate the influential protesters, drastically reduced the new tax rates.[10]

Rivera's action came in response to his central economic-policy dilemma. He sought to gain the strong support of agricultural and business interests while salvaging something of tax reform. He was firmly convinced that without elite support El Salvador's economy would not quickly recover from the 1958 recession and the 1960 political upheaval. By 1963 Rivera succeeded in his campaign to gain elite support, but it came at the expense of new social reforms and most of his tax reforms. The elite, after two years of protest, finally convinced the government that the increased tax burdens proposed by Rivera would impede savings, discourage national and foreign investment, and place Salvadorian business at a disadvantage within the Central American Common Market.[11]

By 1964 the Central American tax reformers had lost many battles, but they still hoped that they could win the long-run tax reform war. Their second opportunity finally came in 1967 and 1968 with the initiation of another round of tax reforms. This time several new conditions appeared to be in the planners' favor. The international agencies, frustrated by what they considered to have been inept management of the earlier reforms, intensified their insistence on concrete tax reform progress. Moreover, the planners were, for the first time, able to make a practical rather than only a theoretical case for reform. In their public investment program reviews in 1966 and 1967 they drew attention to the adverse effects of the decline in import tax revenues resulting from the Common Market tariff reductions. More important, they argued that the five countries, in the aggregate, had experienced chronic fiscal deficits every year of the 1960–67 period. During these years expenditures had risen at a

9. Ibid., no. 35 (October 1961), p. 3.
10. Ibid., no. 36 (December 1961), p. 9.
11. Ibid., no. 42 (June 1963), p.7.

compound rate of 10.2 percent while revenues had increased by only 7.9 percent.[12] In 1965 and 1966 the effects of these fiscal imbalances were seen in the public investment shortcomings of the Five Year Plans. Thus, by early 1967 the stage was set for the long-awaited tax reform initiatives. Or so it appeared.

Guatemalan President Méndez Montenegro, in need of new revenues to compensate for a dramatic revenue decline in 1965 and 1966, boldly initiated new tax reforms in early 1968 at the urging of his planners and Finance Minister. He had little choice but to attempt such reforms, for his conservative Central Bank refused to expand credit to the public sector and international agencies demanded tax reform as a precondition for additional financial assistance. Under the leadership of Finance Minister Alberto Fuentes Mohr, one of Central America's most respected economists, the Guatemalan Congress enacted a 5 percent sales tax and a 20 percent tax on nonessential goods. The new taxes were to be enforced at the wholesale level for the first time, making traditional tax avoidance more difficult.

After signing the controversial measures Méndez was forced into hasty retreat. Protests, similar to those made against Ydígoras' tax reforms five years earlier, were unleased by Guatemala's economic associations. The urban middle class joined in the harassment of the Guatemalan president claiming that, until the enforcement of existing taxes was more consistent and equitable, they would refuse to pay new taxes. Their case was inadvertently supported by the Guatemalan budget director who admitted that "in Guatemala taxes are at the mercy of those who want to pay them, or are paid by those who can't avoid them, like salaried workers."[13]

Under intense pressure, the insecure Méndez rescinded the tax measures less than a month after their passage and forced the resignation of Finance Minister Fuentes Mohr whose strong advocacy of tax reform had made him the target of opposition

12. Joseph Pincus, *Origins and Estimated Effects of the San José Protocol* (San Salvador: USAID, 1968), p. 7.

13. Quoted in OEA Secretaria, *El esfuerzo interno y las necesidades de financiamiento externo para el desarrollo de Guatemala* (Washington, 1969), p. 5.

fury.[14] Fuentes Mohr's replacement, Mario Fuentes Pieruccini, an experienced Revolutionary party politician, attempted to raise tax revenues through more subtle, incremental tax changes during the remainder of 1968. He expanded the traditional stamp tax, increased the tobacco tax, and created a tax on airline tickets. These measures, however, were too small and too late to compensate for the revenue lost by the withdrawal of Méndez's tax reforms.[15]

Like his predecessor Rivera, and much like Méndez in Guatemala, El Salvador's President Fidel Sánchez also failed to implement a tax reform program. In fact, his behavior closely paralleled that of Méndez. Salvadorian leaders had observed Guatemalan events closely since the early nineteenth century. As the Guatemalan government moved leftward in the 1940s, the Salvadorian military organized an authoritarian reform party to prevent similar developments in El Salvador. In late 1967 President Sánchez submitted individual and corporate income tax reforms to his Congress where they gained narrow approval after a long debate in late 1967. But simultaneously with the outburst of opposition to Méndez's tax program in Guatemala, a loud opposition attack on Sánchez's reforms arose in El Salvador. Seeing the besieged Méndez retract his program, Sánchez hastily decided to preserve his upper and middle class support by similarly rescinding his tax reforms in early 1968.[16]

All was not despair in Central America, however, for tax reform did make some headway in Costa Rica. When he was in-

14. Economist Intelligence Unit, *Quarterly Economic Review—Central America*, no. 2 (1968), p. 3.

15. The impact of Méndez's retreat on his development program can be seen in his 1968 budgetary decisions. The central government had received legislative authorization for a budget of $198 million for 1968, but after the tax reform was rescinded this was cut to $178 million. However, by the end of the year the government was able to spend only $167 million. See OEA Secretaria, *El esfuerzo interno . . . Guatemala* (1969), pp. 50–51; and Banco de Guatemala, *Estudio económico y memoria de labores Año 1968* (Guatemala, 1969), pp. 55–63.

16. Data based on interviews (see Note on Sources) and Economist Intelligence Unit, *Quarterly Economic Review—Central America*, no. 3 (1968).

augurated in 1966, conservative President José Trejos encountered the deepest fiscal crisis in the region. Costa Rica's fiscal
problem was, ironically, the product of its government's con-
structive effort to deal with the country's major social problems
after the Revolution in 1948. Very extensive government programs in the fields of education, health, and social assistance
produced a dramatic rise in current expenditures that began
consuming all public revenues and causing large fiscal deficits
after 1964. In seeking to restore fiscal balance, President Trejos
faced two policy alternatives. He could raise revenues through
new or increased taxation or he could reduce expenditures by
imposing strict budgetary austerity. It quickly became apparent
that the second alternative lacked political feasibility, for as
Trejos' planning agency director complained, "the structure of
our budget is such that it is difficult to reduce it . . . more or less
half of the budget goes to hospitals, education and other social
services that receive income set by law; the president or the
legislature can do little to alter this without producing a great
public outcry."[17] Trejos and his planners concluded that his only
viable policy alternative was new taxation. While he did not control a majority in the Costa Rican legislature, he expected the
cooperation of the liberal PLN majority since most of the new
revenue would be used to support the social and economic programs that they had traditionally supported. Consequently, he
was surprised to see his property and sales tax proposals become
entangled for months in a struggle between himself, the legislature and, eventually, the International Monetary Fund. The latter
had insisted on new taxes as a requirement for the additional
compensatory assistance that Costa Rica needed in 1967; nevertheless, the PLN-controlled legislature rejected both tax proposals in order to embarass President Trejos. The impasse was
finally broken in July 1967, when the legislature gave in to international pressures and enacted the sales, but not the property
tax to slowdown the country's surging fiscal crisis.[18]

17. OEA, *Informe final del subcomité del CIAP sobre Costa Rica*
(Washington, 1968), p. 17.
18. Economist Intelligence Unit, *Quarterly Economic Review—Central America*, nos. 1 and 3 (1967).

Despite the enactment of the Costa Rican sales tax, tax reform enjoyed few successes in Central America. With the exception of the decline in import taxes caused by regional tariff agreements, the five countries' tax structures changed little during the decade. In the struggle over tax reform the principal bargaining advantage belonged to its active opponents who successfully threatened to withdraw their economic and political support of the Central American presidents if the reforms were implemented. International agencies, on the other hand, were often forced by their long-range commitments to development projects to disburse their funds despite displeasure over the tax reform failures. The planners threatened that their public investment programs would collapse without the support of new tax revenues, but their threats fell on the deaf ears of presidents who were more concerned with their personal political survival than their marginal development program successes.

What is striking about tax reform in Central America is not so much its unfortunate fate as the way this unpopular intruder was managed by policy-makers. A general pattern of policy-making behavior emerges from these Central American tax reform experiences. First, in response to the demands and advice of their planners and the international agencies, presidents proposed ambitious tax reform legislation. If an opposition party controlled the legislature, the measure was abruptly defeated. But if the president's party dominated, there was extensive debate, delay, and modification of the presidential proposals. Finally, the legislature enacted the measure; but this, in turn, provoked opposition outbursts and presidential withdrawal or modification of the new legislation.

Of particular interest is the openness and visibility of this battle in all of the Central American countries. No longer are revenue policies made covertly by a ruling elite as was common before World War II. Instead, even in these small countries, such policy decisions are surrounded by presidential pronouncements of reform commitments and vitriolic denunciations by the opposition. Of course, some negotiations between the president and his opposition continue covertly, but the importance of the public dramatics should not be missed.

Presidential dramatics are due in part to the new openness of reform politics. At the same time, they may be partially explained by presidential manipulation of countervailing oppositions. Having accepted extensive foreign assistance, a president opens himself to the demands of international agencies who continually insist on tax reform. Since 1960 Central American presidents have been overwhelmed with such reform proposals, many of which were made preconditions of foreign assistance. It was therefore imperative that they make an effort to implement such reforms in order to convince their foreign supporters of their good will. At the same time, however, presidents have been aware of their likely failure to implement such reforms. More important, they have also discovered a convenient scapegoat in these "political realities" that often defeat their reform proposals. Thus, by encouraging public battles over tax reforms, they were able to convince international agencies that, despite sincere presidential intentions, they were forced to yield to inalterable political opposition. In so doing they survived with their foreign support generally secure.[19]

THE USE OF FOREIGN ASSISTANCE

Amid increasing expenditures, lagging revenues, and tax reform failures, foreign financial assistance offered a welcomed means of rescuing Central America's development programs. Planners quite naturally turned to international agencies for moral support, technical advice, and financial assistance. The representatives of international agencies spoke the planners' technical language and supported their programming activities. Most planners admitted feeling they had more in common with Alliance administrators than they did with the more politically motivated Ministers on their own planning councils; in fact, they often yielded to the temptation to retreat into the technical world of elegant econometric models and macroeconomic theory shared

19. This interpretation of presidential behavior is drawn from the historical record and from interviews; see Note on Sources.

by their foreign allies to escape the frustrations they experienced in national policy-making councils.

The international agencies also fit well into the policy designs of Central American presidents. They had assisted in the initiation of development programs in the 1950s and had financed the construction of crucial infrastructure projects. Moreover, the Alliance for Progress offered even greater assistance as the new decade began, tempting new development policy commitments by Central American presidents. Ambitious but unrevolutionary, they recognized the political and economic difficulties of generating all of their needed capital within their own societies and welcomed foreign support as a suitable supplement. This strategy of foreign finance, however, proved quite simplistic when tested by policy-making experience. Two forces, clear perhaps only through hindsight, undermined its utility: the immense long-range financial needs of Central American development programs; and the difficult and often politically unacceptable demands that accompanied foreign support.

Until the recession that began in 1958, development investments were supported primarily by resources generated within Central America. But after 1958 the need for foreign assistance dramatically increased. To compensate for insufficient revenues and foreign exchange reserves Central American presidents sought to coordinate national and foreign financing. That is, they attempted to disburse foreign assistance at moments when adverse fiscal conditions required it. The task was not simple, for Central American presidents controlled neither the timing of fiscal crisis nor the authorization for, and often not even the disbursement of foreign assistance. Thus, despite their intentions, there was often little natural harmony between their needs and their use of foreign assistance. As a result, policy dissynchronization rather than harmonious policy management became the pattern after 1958.

Each national experience reflects a slight variant of this pattern. Costa Rica enlarged its dependence on foreign assistance after its development programs were seriously threatened by the post-1958 recession. But as foreign assistance increased so did national budgets, leaving the Costa Rican fiscal crisis unsolved. Nicaragua successfully imposed austerity policies after 1958 and harmonized its revenue and its borrowing during the first half of the decade, but when fiscal crisis struck in 1968 foreign assistance could not be expanded fast enough to compensate for falling domestic revenues. The Hondurans were just beginning their development program as the post-1958 recession began and suffered many stillborn programs during the Villeda era. Yet when the recession ended and foreign assistance authorizations were accelerated in the mid-1960s, Honduran policy-makers reacted slowly and failed to take advantage of their available resources by rapidly expanding investment programs. The Salvadorians, starting the development decade with a recession and political unrest, disbursed extensive foreign assistance before 1965, but because of internal political opposition to increasing their foreign debt burden and the termination of their recession in the mid-1960s, they reduced its use after 1965. When recession struck again in the late 1960s the unprepared Salvadorian president was forced to make severe cuts in development programs. Guatemala is distinguished from the other countries by the penetration of substantial American assistance into the country in the mid-1950s. This dramatic increase in foreign-financed programs was followed, however, by tragic reductions that coincided with an economic recession in the early 1960s. Development investments were expanded again in the late 1960s only to be curtailed by another recession.

In trying to explain patterns of foreign aid management by national policy-makers, it is clear that need alone did not determine the amount of financial assistance received by the Central American countries. Equally influential were the countries' fiscal strategies, their conformity to the fiscal standards demanded by the international agencies, and their administrative ability to absorb and spend the foreign loans and grants.

The five governments desired foreign assistance, but the intensity of their demands varied according to their fiscal strategies. At one extreme was Costa Rica's very liberal strategy of absorbing all that it could acquire regardless of the long-range financial obligations incurred. The expansionary expenditure policies ini-

obligations incurred. The expansionary expenditure policies initiated by President Figueres between 1954 and 1958 proved irrevocable despite the efforts of conservative regimes to reduce expenditures between 1958 and 1963 and again between 1966 and 1970. Popular political pressures actually forced Costa Rica's conservative regimes to expand rather than contract expenditures. Such pressures partially explain the irony of Costa Rica's receipt of the region's largest annual foreign loan authorization of the decade in 1961 when the conservative Echandi administration received $62.8 million in development and compensatory loan authorizations. (See Table 5.) Equally revealing is Costa Rica's receipt of average per capita authorizations of $14.49 during the 1961–66 period, which far exceeds the Central American average of $5.86. (See also n. 21 on p. 103.)

TABLE 5

Authorizations of Loans by International Agencies, 1961–1967[a]
(Millions of U S $)

	1961	1962	1963	1964	1965	1966	1967	Avg. Author. 1961–66	Avg. Per Cap. Author. 1961–66
			Development Loans						
Costa Rica	41.8	8.5	40.1	10.6	23.1	4.1	6.4	21.4	14.39
El Salvador	15.2	14.2	32.1	9.6	15.3	1.6	3.2	14.7	5.03
Guatemala	13.6	8.8	6.4	7.8	2.7	19.9	32.4	9.9	2.13
Honduras	13.8	10.1	5.2	6.1	27.2	19.2	23.2	13.6	5.80
Nicaragua	8.6	14.8	2.7	10.9	21.4	29.8	10.7	16.4	9.94
Totals and Averages	*93.0*	*56.4*	*86.5*	*45.0*	*89.7*	*74.6*	*75.9*	*15.2*	*5.86*
			Compensatory Loans						
Costa Rica	21.0	14.2	—	—	12.5	10.0	15.5		
El Salvador	23.2	11.2	5.0	—	20.0	—	10.0		
Guatemala	15.0	—	—	—	—	15.0	13.4		
Honduras	7.5	7.5	7.5	7.5	—	10.0	—		
Nicaragua	—	—	11.2	11.2	—	—	—		
Totals	*66.7*	*32.9*	*23.7*	*18.7*	*32.5*	*35.0*	*38.9*		

[a] Included are: USAID, Export-Import Bank, World Bank Group, Inter-American Development Bank, and the Central American Bank for Economic Integration.

Source: OEA, *El avance de la integración centroamericana y las necesidades de financiamiento externo* (Washington, 1968), Anexo A, p. 103.

El Salvador occupies the opposite extreme. The Salvadorian government had long followed a conservative fiscal policy under the urging of the country's watchful economic elite. During the 1950s, for example, the Salvadorians accepted fewer and smaller loans from international agencies than any of their neighbors. Under the Alliance they received average annual authorizations of $17.2 million between 1961 and 1965 but in 1966 and 1967 combined they received only $4.8 million. This reduction came as emerging opposition parties, aware of the expansion of foreign borrowing by President Rivera under the Alliance, used the old issue of fiscal responsibility against the government. Their opposition was especially effective after the 1966 election in which they captured over one-third of the congressional seats and the power to block the ratification of foreign loan agreements.

Guatemalan policy fluctuated between the two extremes as it did on so many issues. Under Colonel Peralta, who took power from Ydígoras in 1963, budgetary austerity was imposed and virtually no new financial assistance was accepted. Peralta viewed himself as a caretaker, not a populist or developer, and he signed fewer new foreign loans in three-and-one-half years than Ydígoras had in two. President Méndez, in contrast, vigorously renewed the signing of loans after his inauguration in 1966. To compensate for a revenue decline caused by a mild recession and to build a popular base for his Revolutionary party, he signed more Alliance loans in his first eighteen months than had his two predecessors in five years.

The amount of financial assistance received by each Central American government was also influenced by its ability to conform to the fiscal policy standards demanded by international agencies. The agencies uniformly insisted upon "fiscal responsibility," by which they meant the avoidance of large fiscal deficits and unmanageable debt obligations. The enforcement of these standards produced some of the most interesting ironies of the decade. Nowhere is this more apparent than in the treatment of Nicaragua and Costa Rica by Alliance administrators. Because of its social welfare programs and political democracy, Costa Rica began the decade as an Alliance showcase, while authoritarian Nicaragua appeared hostile ground for the realization of most Alliance objectives. But the Nicaraguans were aware of the expectations of Alliance administrators and adroitly initiated enough welfare programs to secure their receipt of ample financial assistance under the Alliance. At the same time, they made fiscal responsibility a major component of their development program, regardless of the consequences for welfare policy. The Nicaraguans impressed international agencies as they demonstrated in the mid-1960s that their conservative fiscal policy, infrastructure investments, and efficient commercial agriculture were yielding the highest GDP growth rate in the region.[20] In contrast to Nicaragua, Costa Rica suffered continual fiscal crises throughout the decade because of its burdensome welfare programs, and by the mid-1960s Alliance administrators began losing confidence in the Costa Ricans. After 1965, in fact, they substantially reduced loan authorizations and demanded that the Costa Ricans put their financial house in order by imposing fiscal austerity. Thus, the Somozas of Nicaragua received extensive financial assistance because they adhered symbolically to Alliance ideals while using their strong presidential power to impose a conservative fiscal policy and control the details of policy implementation. The Costa Ricans, in contrast, incurred the wrath of Alliance administrators because they were unable to fund many Alliance projects due to the fiscal burdens imposed by their social programs. Most revealing in the two cases is the irony in the satisfaction of international agencies with the performance of an authoritarian regime and their dissatisfaction with a democratic one.[21]

20. For example in 1966 a World Bank official said in praise of the Nicaraguan government: "Its record has been very good in the past and we are confident that its possibilities are good. We have always been impressed with the stability of Nicaraguan currency and fiscal administration and we have always viewed its low external debt with great satisfaction." Quoted in OEA, *Informe final del subcomité del CIAP sobre Nicaragua* (Washington, 1967), p. 31.

21. Guatemala's receipt of the least foreign assistance during the decade deserves some explanation. In contrast to the large amounts of assistance that Guatemala received in the mid-1950s, it received only a $5.03 annual per capita average during the 1960s because of US disenchantment with Guatemalan leadership in the early 1960s, a petty but

A final factor that influenced the amount of financial assistance was the ability of the recipient government to utilize its loans. One might assume that the spending of money would offer few problems to an impoverished government that desires rapid development. Actually, the opposite is frequently the case. The disbursement of funds often lags far behind their appropriation because of the recipient's failure to meet such loan requirements as matching funds, or because of delays in the designing of the project or, even more commonly, due to the bureaucracy's inability to implement the project. While common to all five countries, the disbursement problem is most clearly illustrated by the experience of Honduras.

In 1965 the stage was set for a long-awaited expansion of Honduran public investment. Foreign loan authorizations, which had been delayed during the first two years of the Alliance, finally began to flow in 1964 and 1965, public revenues were rapidly expanding for the first time in over a decade, and the 1965–69 Honduran Five Year Plan was ready for implementation. Honduran planners were convinced that their big opportunity had finally arrived. But the Hondurans missed that opportunity. The public investment program did not take off but crept along at its usual slow pace. The massive infusion of foreign assistance did not produce dynamic projects as expected because loan disbursement was obstructed by the Hondurans' incapacity to manage an increased volume of operations. Consequently, while loan authorizations were increasing, disbursements, which should have been expanded proportionately, were declining. After having risen to $16.4 million in 1963, foreign loan disbursements actually dropped to $10.3 million in 1965 and $8.8 million in 1966.[22]

Despite all of the obstacles and conditions that produced different authorization and disbursement patterns in the five coun-

---

harmful dispute with the World Bank which held up numerous loans until the late 1960s, and Peralta's reluctance to assume new debts between 1963 and 1967.

22. OAS Secretariat, *Domestic Efforts and the Needs for External Financing for Development in Honduras* (Washington, 1967), p. 136.

tries, they could still credit foreign financial assistance with the stimulation and support of most of their development projects. The planners' implementation of only half of their public investment objectives was disappointing, to be sure, but the disappointment would have been much greater were it not for the support they received from foreign loans and grants.

The Central American experience revals the complexity of applying foreign assistance to national-development programs. Aid does not simply flow like water from a faucet into an empty glass. Instead, numerous internal and external conditions interact to determine the targets and amount of foreign assistance. It appears that to intiate requests for assistance a government must begin with a liberal borrowing policy, yet to receive it continually it must follow a rather conservative fiscal policy. To combine the two is an extremely difficult task requiring, among other things, firm presidential control of policy-making and favorable economic conditions. As we have seen, Costa Rica pursued the liberal borrowing policy but not the conservative fiscal policy, while in El Salvador the reverse was true. Nicaragua and Honduras managed to combine the two, yet the Hondurans failed to provide the responsive implementation machinery that is required to realize the benefits of foreign assistance. Ironically, it was in authoritarian Nicaragua, where the planners were almost totally ignored, that these three conditions were combined most effectively.

A REGIONAL RESPONSE TO CRISIS

Central America's fiscal policy-making environment began to change after the initiation of regional economic integration in 1958. Integration required the abolition of tariffs on most commodities in intra-regional trade. After the signing of the General Treaty in 1961 over 74 percent of all items listed in the Central American tariff schedule became entitled to free trade. Within the following five years, another 20 percent was added to the free list, so that by the end of 1966 approximately 94 percent were exempt from import duties within the Common Market.

Cotton, coffee, and sugar remained outside the agreements, but the latter two were subject to national quotas fixed by international accords.[23]

Initially, only the economic benefits of integration were clearly perceived by Central American policy-makers. Their goal of trade expansion was quickly realized as the value of intra-regional trade increased from $32.7 million in 1960 to $173.9 million in 1966.[24] During the same period Central American export prices improved, regional GDP (Gross Domestic Product) growth rates averaged approximately 6 percent, and the region substantially recovered from its 1957 recession. Then, quite suddenly, a new array of economic crises gripped the entire region. But this time a new variable, regional integration, was part of both their cause and their solution.

The region's principal economic crisis, while reflected in numerous indices, was most clearly revealed by balance of payments and fiscal conditions. The international liquidity position of Central American Central Banks had declined during the recession of the late 1950s and early 1960s only to rise again to a new peak of $224.7 million in 1965.[25] Then, in 1967 they came full cycle as their liquidity position deteriorated to $195.3 million, a decline of 13 percent from the 1965 level. Similarly, the foreign asset position of the region's Central Banks also declined after 1965 because of the steep rise in the foreign liabilities of deposit money banks. By 1967 the net foreign assets of the Central American banking system aggregated only $22.2 million, or less than one-fourth of the peak achieved in 1963. This extremely dangerous level of net foreign assets in relation to high import levels—let alone total foreign exchange requirements for balance of payment transactions— convinced Central American policy-makers that their international asset earning capacity was

---

23. Roger D. Hansen, *Central America: Regional Integration and Economic Development* (Washington: National Planning Association, 1967), p. 136.

24. OEA, *El avance de la integratión centroamericano*, Anexo C, p. 93.

25. I am using here the International Monetary Fund definition of Central Bank international reserve liquidity, which is the sum of its gross holdings of gold and foreign exchange plus its IMF gold tranche position.

most inadequate to support the higher import levels needed to sustain a minimum satisfactory rate of economic growth. In fact, if the sharply rising net liability position of commercial banks went unchecked, the credit position of all Central American importers vis-à-vis their foreign suppliers would be seriously impaired.[26]

To compound their problems, Central American policy-makers also faced deteriorating fiscal conditions after 1965. As we have seen, import taxes as a percentage of import value and total government revenue declined significantly after the implementation of the Common Market tariff agreements. Moreover, attempts at structural tax reform were frequently obstructed and consequently failed to supply adequate compensation for the reduction in tariff revenues. Fiscal conditions finally reached crisis proportions between 1965 and 1967 when the five governments' public expenditures rose by 20 percent while their revenues increased by only 8 percent, producing serious fiscal imbalances in all five countries.[27] Most painful in the short run, they were forced to postpone their use of some foreign loans because of their inability to supply sufficient local currencies to match loans intended to support public investment programs.

With their new Five Year Plans suddenly in jeopardy, Central American planners sought immediate remedies. The first to offer them suggestions were the international agencies that had always been ready with advice. In conformity with their traditional support of fiscal orthodoxy, they urged a policy of strict fiscal austerity to restore financial stability to the region and, under the leadership of the International Monetary Fund, they sought to use their offers of loans and compensatory financing as leverage in inducing compliance with their advice. Despite their vulnerability to external financial pressures, however, Central American policy-makers did not give in to these demands because they faced numerous internal obstacles to such reductions in public expenditures. Many of their budgetary obligations were determined by legal and constitutional requirements that could

26. Pincus, *Origins . . . San José Protocol*, pp. 1–3.
27. OEA, *El avance de la integratión centroamericana*, Anexo C, p. 46.

not be changed without legislative approval. More seriously, they faced popular opposition to reductions in public employment and development programs. Public employment had grown dramatically in the 1950s as new agencies were created and governmental services extended. Operating expenditures rose rapidly to support bureaucratic expansion and sustain services for a growing urban population. Central American presidents recognized these pressures and, with the exception of the Somozas, they proposed much austerity yet produced very little. Take the Costa Ricans, for example. They continually failed to comply with most of the austerity requirements of their agreements with the IMF because of popular political constraints on their budgetary reductions. Yet, while earning persistent IMF condemnation, they managed until near the end of the decade, when the disillusionment of the international agencies caught up with them, to secure extensive foreign financial support while imposing only the mildest of austerity measures.

The Nicaraguans, in contrast to the other four countries, did succeed in imposing firm austerity in the face of a fiscal crisis in 1968. Their relative freedom in doing so deserves some explanation. Authoritarian President Anastasio Somoza, Jr., unlike most of his Central American counterparts, was not constrained by large welfare policy commitments or activist lower and middle class political forces. In fact, the Somozas had conspicuously avoided the cultivation of both. As a result, President Somoza was able to impose both severe budget cuts and a sales tax in 1968.

Austerity budgets proved an inadequate means of coping with fiscal crises, so Central American policy-makers searched elsewhere for feasible policy alternatives in 1968. Leading the search were each nation's economic planners and Ministers of Economy. The planners, as usual, were confronted by a perplexing problem. On the one hand, the existing fiscal crisis threatened their development programs, for it denied them the local curriencies they needed to match foreign development loans. On the other hand, the austerity solution, while eventually yielding foreign confidence and new loans, threatened the short-run implementation of their development programs.

They did not despair for long, however, for a solution to their dilemma soon emerged. Of their three possible policy choices—austerity, continued crisis, or revenue expansion—the latter still appeared the most viable alternative despite its discouraging past record. The use of new revenue policy initiatives was suggested to the planners by the region's frustrated and anxious Ministers of Economy who saw such use primarily as a side effect of their program for dealing with balance of payments crises. Their program emerged from a series of meetings of the regional Economic Council in late 1967 and early 1968. Known as the "San José" Protocol to the General Treaty of Economic Integration, it called for the levying of certain tax measures as a short-run solution to balance of payments and fiscal problems. The key provisions, which were to remain in force for five years included: a 30 percent surcharge on the amount of import tariffs paid on all but a specific list of imports from outside the Common Market area; and a one-stage consumption tax of 20 and 10 percent on specified commodities.[28]

It was generally believed that the Protocol's most impressive feature was its political acceptability, for it was offered to the Central American economic elites as a compelling and less costly alternative to a renewal of tax reform initiatives. But, despite these assumptions, the Protocol, which required ratification by three of five governments to become effective, encountered major obstacles and stimulated new policy conflicts in national and regional policy-making arenas. The Costa Ricans refused to ratify it, the Nicaraguans implemented it before the required three governments had ratified it, and the Hondurans had to impose a state of seige in order to assure its promulgation.

Costa Rican President Trejos, as we have seen, sought to solve Costa Rica's fiscal crisis through the enactment of new sales and property taxes but succeeded only with the former after a long struggle with the PLN opposition in the Costa Rican legislature. Still in need of new revenues, he siezed the Protocol as a new opportunity to generate such revenues. But once again he encountered congressional opposition. This time the PLN deputies

28. Pincus, *Origins . . . San José Protocol*, p. 5.

justified their obstructionist tactics by arguing that the Protocol taxes were too regressive. In exchange for its passage the deputies demanded the promulgation of more progressive income tax legislation. But Trejos and his conservative supporters refused to submit or sign such legislation and, consequently, the Protocol was not ratified by the Costa Ricans.

Nicaragua's more authoritarian President Somoza, in contrast to the severely constrained Trejos, imposed the Protocol without awaiting ratification by two other governments as required. Somoza claimed that Nicaragua had suffered more than the other Central American governments from the creation of the Common Market because its industries were unable to compete with those of the other countries. In addition, he claimed that Nicaragua had lost $122 million in tariff revenues between 1965 and 1968. To demonstrate his displeasure and resolve his fiscal crisis, he ignored regional agreements and imposed the Protocol surcharge and, as if that were insufficient, added consumption taxes on items produced within the Common Market. These impulsive, unilateral actions threw the Common Market Secretariat into a frenzy throughout the remainder of 1968.[29]

Honduran President López provoked unexpected opposition when he tried to implement the Protocol. Communication between the Honduran president and the Honduran masses had traditionally been weak and generally unnecessary since few economic policies were ever intended for mass consumption. While the Protocol was directed entirely at imported goods, false rumors about its application to all internal commerce were circulated by President López's opposition. The opposition charge that prices on all consumption items would rise after the promulgation of the Protocol prompted protests in market places throughout the country. Unable to communicate the Protocol's actual objectives and instruments, López finally was forced to impose a state of siege to suppress his strongest critics, the banana plantation workers and the merchants on Honduras' north coast.

The urgency of Protocol ratification was particularly acute in

29. Economist Intelligence Unit, *Quarterly Economic Review—Central America*, no. 3 (1968); Banco Central de Nicaragua, *Informe Económico—1968* (Managua, 1969).

Guatemala and El Salvador in mid-1968. As will be recalled, tax reforms were rescinded in both countries in the face of concerted opposition. As a result, both governments suffered fiscal crises during 1968. Policy-makers in both countries siezed the Protocol as the most feasible means of compensating for their tax reform failures. To their surprise, commercial and agricultural interests were quite restrained in their opposition to the Protocol, for after much debate they accepted official arguments supporting it as an alternative to new reform initiatives. With its ratification by Guatemala and El Salvador in late 1968 the Protocol officially became the region's first coordinated response to the problem of resource mobilization.

Many observers considered the San José Protocol a bold new policy departure that inaugurated a new era of development policy-making throughout the region. But, as so often was the case, their optimism was undermined by another Central American crisis.

In July 1969 Central America's strides toward unity were shattered by the outbreak of war between Honduras and El Salvador. The military conflict lasted only two weeks thanks to the effective intervention of the Organization of American States, but hostilities were channelled into economic sanctions during the remainder of 1969. The Hondurans blocked the Inter-American Highway, El Salvador's principal trade link with Nicaragua and Costa Rica, which traverses a small section of southern Honduras. In addition, the Hondurans terminated their trade with El Salvador, which had enjoyed a favorable trade balance of $17.2 million with Honduras in 1968. Amid broken trade flows the Common Market Secretariat spent the remainder of 1969 frantically, but unsuccessfully, trying to restore political and economic order throughout the region.

The causes of the conflict are more clearly apparent than its long range consequences. Intra-regional conflict had been common to the region throughout its modern history. The migration of an estimated 300,000 Salvadorians during the past 30 years across the undemarcated frontier from densely populated El Salvador to underpopulated Honduras had long been a source of friction between the two countries. In June 1969 the Honduran government's expulsion of Salvadorian squatters from government lands intended for use in the Honduran agrarian reform program touched off violent clashes between spectators at two Salvadorian-Honduran soccer matches. Responding to what it perceived as Honduran threats to the safety and property of Salvadorians residing in Honduras, the Salvadorian army invaded Honduras in mid-July but was stopped short just inside Honduran territory when the OAS intervened.[30]

The impact of the conflict on development policy-making was felt immediately in Honduras and El Salvador. Honduran planners dropped all supervision of their Five Year Plan and concentrated on an Emergency Plan for the war-torn area during the remainder of 1969. Moreover, they redirected their public investments from planned projects to emergency programs to aid the victims of the conflict. Similarly, the Salvadorian president began to reorder his public investment priorities. Although already unable to supply services and employment for many of his countrymen, President Sánchez nevertheless proposed a special development plan to aid the several thousand Salvadorian refugees who poured back into El Salvador from Honduras. His program was cut short, however, as scarce public revenues were first channelled into the rearmament of the Salvadorian Army and Air Force.

The Honduran-Salvadorian conflict was another reminder of the conditions that have long obstructed regional development in Central America. In the short run it distracted resources and policy-makers from their difficult tasks of development policy-making and regional cooperation. But despite its ferocity and the ill-will that it rekindled, it did not destroy the region's development programs. Like so many uninvited intruders before it, the "Soccer War" of 1969 only slowed the already gradual pace of Central American development.

30. For more details on the Honduran-Salvadorian conflict see: Vincent Cable, "The 'Football War' and the Central American Common Market," *International Affairs* 45 (October 1969): 658–71; J. S. Nye, *Peace in Parts: Integration and Conflict in Regional Organization* (Boston: Little Brown, 1971), pp. 117–23; and *The Washington Post* and *The New York Times* for July and August, 1969.

PATTERNS OF PUBLIC EXPENDITURE

Until now we have focused only on the process of revenue mobilization, but to understand the consequences of revenue policy-making during the 1960s, we must examine its impact on public expenditures. Of particular interest is the fate of the region's Five Year Plans which operated under the numerous revenue policy constraints described above.

Quite clearly, the planners' development programs were the principal victims of the revenue policy shortcomings that prevailed during the decade. This is most clearly seen in the fate of their public investment programs. The planners had hoped to build upon the development programs of the 1950s by expanding public investments even more in the 1960s. But they fell short of their objective, for while the Central American governments had increased their public investments by 300 percent from $35.4 to $104.5 million between 1950 and 1957, they managed an increase of only 75 percent, from $72.5 to $126.3 million between 1960 and 1967.[31]

The public sector's share of the Central American economy had always been small. But guided by their development strategies, the planners sought to stimulate national economic development by expanding the government's share of the GNP. Only in Costa Rica and Nicaragua, however, was their success more than marginal; in Guatemala the public sector's share actually declined. The same pattern holds true for the ratio of public investment to GNP; Costa Rica's increase of 1 percent was the region's largest while Honduras' 0.3 percent was the smallest. (See Table 6.)

Perhaps the best indicator of public investment performance is the record of the five governments' 1965–69 Five Year Plans. In Figure No. 2 actual investments (solid line) are compared with planned investments (broken line) in the five countries. The obvious failure of each government to fulfill its public investment

31. OEA, *El avance de la integración centroamericana*, Anexo C, Cuadro I-6.

TABLE 6
Central Government Expenditures and Public Investment
as a Percent of GNP

	Total CG Expenditures			Public Investment		
	1960	*1963*	*1966*	*1960*	*1963*	*1966*
Costa Rica	14.1	16.2	19.1	3.3	4.1	4.3
El Salvador	10.9	9.9	11.0	2.8	2.5	3.7
Guatemala	11.0	10.7	10.7	2.1	1.4	2.9
Honduras	11.5	10.7	13.5	2.7	3.4	2.4
Nicaragua	10.9	11.4	14.6	3.0	4.4	3.7

Source: Computed from OEA, *El avance de la integración centroamericana y las necesidades de financiamiento externo* (Washington, 1968), Anexo A, pp. 31–37, 41–46.

goals is quite clear. This shortcoming, however, should not be too surprising. Public investment objectives are seldom attained in new planning systems, particularly in ones like Central America's where the Five Year Plans were hurriedly designed under severe data constraints. Moreover, Central American planners readily admit that they were forced to base their projections on "guesstimates" of their public investment potential. But if the fact that they did not reach their lofty goals is not totally surprising, their failure to expand public investments any more than they did is surprising. Most striking is the relative consistency of public investment levels despite efforts to increase them. This raises the obvious question of why public investments uniformly followed such a pattern. That is, what conditions influenced these patterns and prevented a significant expansion of public investment after 1964?

Part of the answer lies in the variables that form what might be termed the public investment decision sequence. A government's public investment is the product of the interaction of several conditions and policy decisions. Looking at it analytically, we begin with the condition of GNP growth; to this is added the tax structure's ability to tap that growth for an increase in public revenues. The third condition, public revenues, is then matched with the fourth, current operating expenditures to yield a fifth, public savings. Before allocating public savings to public

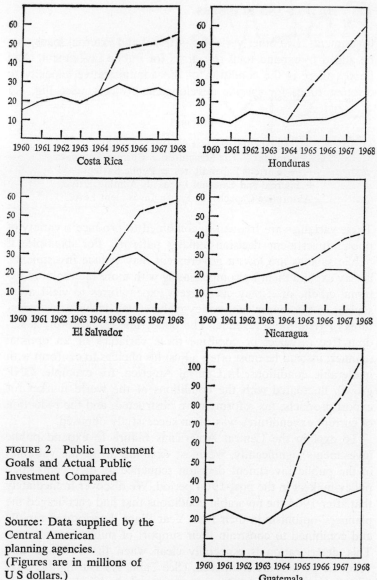

FIGURE 2 Public Investment Goals and Actual Public Investment Compared

Source: Data supplied by the Central American planning agencies. (Figures are in millions of U S dollars.)

investments, two other variables, internal and external loans, can be added to expand total resources for public investment. And finally, there is the condition of the administrative capacity to disburse funds for specific development projects. (See Fig. 3.)

(See Fig. 3.)

FIGURE 3

PUBLIC INVESTMENT DECISION SEQUENCE

GNP Growth + Tax Structures = Current Revenues
− Current Expenditures = Public Savings
+ Internal and External Loans + Administrative
Absorptive Capacity = Public Investment Level

These variables are frequently combined to produce a variety of public investment decision-making patterns. For example, if public savings are low, a government may reduce investments, it may expand them by compensating with more internal and external credit, or it may cut current expenditures to yield more saving. In the longer run, policy-makers may reshape tax structures to yield more revenue. The policy-maker, however, is seldom free to select or combine these variables in an optimal manner; instead he must often adjust his choices to conform with inalterable conditions. In Central America, for example, GNP growth fluctuated with the conditions of the world market for export products, tax reforms were obstructed, and the reduction of current expenditures was often successfully opposed.

To explain the Central Americans failure to expand public investments significantly, we must examine all of the variables in the public investment decision sequence as they confronted policy-makers in the post-1964 period. We discover immediately that after 1964 the favorable conditions that had encouraged the planners' optimism in their Five Year Plans deteriorated rapidly and combined to constrain their support of public investments. This deterioration is especially clear when the 1960–65 and 1965–67 periods are compared. (See Table 7.) During the latter period the region's rate of economic growth declined and the rate of revenue growth dropped by more than half. Current expenditures, however, expanded at a higher rate and absorbed greater proportions of total public revenues. As a result, public savings

TABLE 7
Average Annual Growth Rates

Variables	1960–1965 %	1965–1967 %
Gross National Product	6.3	4.1
Public Sector Current Revenue	8.6	3.8
Public Sector Current Expenditures	7.3	9.2
Public Savings	15.0	−26.0
Internal Loan Disbursed	7.8	− 4.0
External Loan Disbursed	30.0	− 2.2

Source: Computed from OEA, *El avance de la integración centroamericana y las necesidades de financiamiento externo* (Washington, 1968), Anexo A, pp. 31–138.

declined dramatically throughout the region after 1964. To the disappointment of Central American policy-makers, internal and external borrowing could not be expanded rapidly enough to compensate for the decline in public saving. Moreover, the region's administrative capacity, while impossible to measure precisely, was insufficient for the absorption of public investment funds and the scheduled implementation of projects. Consequently, under these adverse economic, financial, and administrative conditions, the Central American planners found it impossible to execute the public investment expansion they so intensely desired.

To be sure, the Central American governments did manage to make many public investments during the 1960s despite the numerous obstacles they confronted. Numerous development projects were completed during the decade in which the planners, their presidents, and the international agencies could take pride. But in the process of implementing their Five Year Plans the Central American planners were forced to tolerate the traditional policy-making processes of which they were only a small part. Moreover, they discovered a gamut of interrelated economic, fiscal, and political conditions which, in the short run at least, they could not change.

The planners encountered fewer obstacles to their influencing of the distribution of public investment than they did in raising

TABLE 8   Costa Rica

	1960 Actual %	1965–69 Plan %	1966 Actual %
Transportation	57	35	16
Electric Energy	16	16	18
Telecommunication	–	8	2
Education	13	7	8
Health	9	15	13
Housing	2	14	8
Other	3	5	35
Total	*100*	*100*	*100*

TABLE 9   El Salvador

	1960 Actual %	1965–69 Plan %	1966 Actual %
Transportation	50	20	12
Electric Energy	9	10	11
Telecommunications	–	4	18
Education	3	9	11
Health	7	15	5
Housing	10	25	10
Other	21	17	33
Total	*100*	*100*	*100*

TABLE 10   Guatemala

	1960 Actual %	1965–69 Plan %	1966 Actual %
Transportation	36	30	28
Electric Energy	1	16	11
Telecommunications	1	4	4
Education	11	4	7
Health	15	15	15
Housing	–	8	7
Other	36	23	28
Total	*100*	*100*	*100*

TABLE 11   Honduras

	1960 Actual %	1965–69 Plan %	1966 Actual %
Transportation	55	38	40
Electric Energy	6	11	10
Telecommunications	–	4	–
Education	3	4	5
Health	10	12	19
Housing	1	5	3
Other	25	26	23
Total	*100*	*100*	*100*

TABLE 12   Nicaragua

	1960 Actual %	1965–69 Plan %	1966 Actual %
Transportation	64	33	50
Electric Energy	8	14	13
Telecommunications	–	3	–
Education	–	6	3
Health	16	12	7
Housing	6	15	7
Other	6	17	20
Total	*100*	*100*	*100*

TABLE 13   Central America

	1960 Actual %	1965–69 Plan %	1966 Actual %
Transportation	49	30	29
Electric Energy	4	14	13
Telecommunications	4	4	9
Education	8	6	7
Health	13	14	15
Housing	3	13	8
Other	19	19	19
Total	*100*	*100*	*100*

Source: Computed from OEA, *El avance de la integración centro-americana* and unpublished data supplied by the Central American planning agencies.

its level. But their investment distribution objectives were also much less ambitious, for they departed only slightly from the public investment priorities that had prevailed throughout the region since the early 1950s. The region's development needs were still quite basic despite the contributions of numerous development projects during the previous decade. Economic infrastructure, especially transportation and electric power, still topped the list of investment targets as they had done a decade earlier. However, the planners did propose some minor changes as we can see by comparing their plans with actual investments made in 1960. (See Tables 8–13.) In the region as a whole, they sought to reduce transport investment slightly while increasing the proportion allocated to electric energy and telecommunications. Social infrastructure was again relegated to a secondary role, although they did propose some expansion of public housing.

Since they planned to distribute their public investments rather evenly over the five years of their plans, we can roughly estimate their influence on allocations by comparing their plan proposals with their actual investments in 1966, a typical year under the plans. Regionally, they managed, as intended, to reduce highway investment and raise that allocated to electric energy and telecommunications. In the social area they reached all objectives except the increase in the proportion allocated to housing. The singular failure of public housing is explained, in part, by the policy-makers' sacrifice of their low priority, newly initiated housing projects when confronted by revenue shortages. Their selection of housing as the first item to be reduced in times of fiscal crisis will be examined in more detail in Chapters 5 and 6.

Cross-national comparisons also reveal some interesting allocative patterns. In Costa Rica and El Salvador, the region's smallest countries and also the two most benefited by the Inter-American Highway, transport investment dropped significantly between 1960 and 1966 while in less developed and larger Nicaragua and Honduras it was still higher than planned. In the social area education, particularly school construction, received a larger proportion than planned in all countries except Nicaragua. The most disappointing social investment performances are found in Nicaragua and El Salvador, the two nations which, as we have seen, pursued the most conservative fiscal policies in the region. In both cases health and housing investments were the first cut in the face of revenue problems in the post-1964 period, while high priority economic infrastructure projects received more support than planned in both countries despite their fiscal problems.

The distribution of total central government expenditures did not change significantly in any of the five countries between 1960 and 1966. (See Table 14.) Here again the priorities of the pre-

TABLE 14
Distribution of Total Central Government Expenditures

	Economic[a] %		Social[b] %		Defense %	
	1960	*1966*	*1960*	*1966*	*1960*	*1966*
Costa Rica[c]	17.5	17.5	22.2	22.6	3.5	2.4
El Salvador	19.3	20.7	41.9	44.9	9.8	10.3
Guatemala	37.6	38.5	27.7	24.6	8.2	9.9
Honduras	28.1	23.7	28.5	39.0	8.4	9.8
Nicaragua	22.3	32.1	20.7	23.5	18.7	12.7

[a] Includes agriculture, industry, transportation and communications.
[b] Includes education, health, social assistance.
[c] The Costa Rican figures are at least 15 percent lower than actual because central government transfers to the numerous semi-autonomous agencies are not included in the Costa Rican computations.
Source: OEA, *El avance de la integración centroamericana y las necesidades de financiamiento externo* (Washington, 1968), Anexo A, pp. 47–51.

ceding decade were continued. Moreover, most of the new government agencies had been created by 1960 and most of the rapid personnel growth had been concluded. Most striking in the central government budgets is the predominance of social over economic expenditures in all countries except Nicaragua. This does not indicate the existence of well-financed, widespread social programs, for the social programs are grossly inadequate in all five countries. Instead, it only points out the comparative high cost of operating national school systems and hospitals in comparison with the cost of operations in the agriculture and economic ministries.

Nicaragua stands out once again because of its relative inattention to social programs. In comparing its low ranking in social programs with the Nicaraguans' successful mobilization of foreign assistance, we are reminded of the difficulty of judging a country's total development program performance because of the contrasting criteria that encourage conflicting evaluations. On the one hand the Nicaraguans skillfully secured and disbursed extensive financial aid, pursued a firm and conservative fiscal policy, and stimulated a rapidly growing economy until the recession that began in 1968. At the same time, they postponed badly needed social programs and, failing to benefit sufficiently from the Common Market, they flagrantly violated regional treaties.

THE LIMITS OF FISCAL POLICY

In raising revenues to support their development programs during the 1960s, Central American presidents struggled to overcome numerous obstacles. Their unstable export economies confronted them with continual uncertainty and the new Common Market reduced one of their traditional revenue resources. They sought to compensate for these adverse conditions by using new fiscal policy instruments to tap new sources of revenue. Persistently, however, they failed to fulfill budgetary needs and development program requirements. Their failure is due, in part, to the conflicting demands of planners who wished to expand programs and the traditional oligarchies and commercial groups who refused to supply the new revenues needed to cover additional expenditures.

The traditional oligarchies were especially opposed to redistributive revenue policies and vigorously obstructed presidential use of new revenue policy instruments, such as the income tax, and of the expanded use of traditional instruments, such as the property tax. Their influence over development policy was linked to their control over the export economy and presidential dependence on their contributions to economic growth. Because of their importance in the national economy, the landed oligarchies often forced presidents to yield to their demands. In the Salvadorian and Guatemalan cases, for example, they successfully opposed tax reforms and forced fiscal crises on their already beleaguered presidents. Moreover, they have persistently forced policy-makers to depend on traditional import, export, stamp, and other regressive transaction taxes, none of which has yielded sufficient revenues nor permitted much policy-making flexibility.

The impact of revenue policy reform failures was aggravated by the insatiable demands of planners and ambitious bureaucrats. The bureaucratic growth and program expansion initiated by reform presidents in the early 1950s suddenly became a liability in the 1960s, for by voraciously consuming revenues and continually demanding more resources, the public agencies often blocked the application of austerity measures and forced extensive use of foreign credit. Manifestations of these liabilities are abundant. Perhaps the most distressing case was that of Costa Rican Presidents Orlich and Trejos who were trapped between the demands of the IMF for fiscal austerity and their planners and bureaucrats for expanded operations and programs. In the end they satisfied neither the IMF nor their planners.

As we know, resource constraints and rigidities have not completely immobilized development policy execution in Central America, for foreign assistance temporarily rescued Central American policy-makers from their resource constraints. At the urging of ambitious reformers, and later the planners, presidents expanded their use of such assistance as rapidly as their fiscal strategies, the international agencies, and their administrative capacities would permit. Foreign assistance, however, did not liberate policy-makers from their domestic constraints in the long run. In fact, it only accentuated their awareness of these constraints. Initially, they mistakenly believed that foreign assistance would resolve their budgetary dilemmas, but they soon discovered that in using the assistance they were actually increasing their resource problems. The purpose of foreign assistance was development project expansion and new projects required new agency operations, which, in turn, demanded additional budgetary support. To complicate matters, rising amortization payments on foreign loans added to the drain on scarce financial resources. Thus, temporary fiscal relief in the early 1960s produced greater budgetary obligations and development policy disappointments in the late 1960s.

5

Planners, Programs, and the Bureaucracy

THE DESIGNING OF DEVELOPMENT PLANS and the allocation of resources are necessary but not sufficient conditions for the realization of development policy objectives. Equally important is the implementation of policy by national bureaucracies. The planner's task does not terminate with his assertion of influence over presidential policy choices, but extends to the supervision of the bureaucratic management of public investments. The implementation task is often even more frustrating than that of influencing policy choices, for although planners may try to affect bureaucratic performance by means of budgetary support, the allocation of new personnel, or close surveillance, they remain to a large extent at the mercy of the capacity, or incapacity, of their administrative agencies.[1]

Few problems frustrated the Central American planners more

1. Policy implementation is much discussed but seldom closely examined in Latin America. Critics of Latin American development programming often blame administrators for the shortcomings of development plans. But such accusations, while well intended, beg the principal questions of why and how policies are obstructed during the implementation process. Instead of simply introducing administrative incompetence as an explanatory variable of last resort, I intend to examine the effects of specific administrative behavior patterns on policy implementation.

than what they called "bureaucratic obstruction" of development programs. At the same time, all planners expressed the belief that, unlike the obstacles caused by political decision-makers, those caused by bureaucratic obstruction were amenable to change through the intervention of the planning agencies. Consequently, they persistently sought to enhance the efficiency of policy implementation by reshaping and reforming their bureaucracies.

In order to focus the examination of the planners efforts to reform Central American administrative behavior, two types of public investment policies have been selected for intense study—highways and public housing. The former represents economic infrastructure investment and the latter social welfare. Their differences offer an opportunity to explore contrasting performance demands and bureaucratic responses. Highways are part of the traditional responsibility of public works ministries while public housing is administered by new autonomous agencies; highways have been high priority items in development programs while housing has received lower priority; and while participants in the market economy are the principal clientele of highway agencies, the urban poor are the principal users of public housing.

I will examine bureaucratic change and performance by concentrating on the organizational structures and operating characteristics of public agencies. The response of organizational structure to new demands is apparent in the success or failure of reorganizations of public agencies. Formal reorganization has been the principal means of bureaucratic adjustment and has served the diverse needs of administrators and political leaders in managing demands for rapid change. I will examine the stimulants and goals of reorganization and obstacles to its successful implementation. Operating characteristics will be examined in terms of the growth or change of program responsibilities and the means of managing these responsibilities. Specifically, I will focus on the allocation of personnel and money and on the organization's acquisition of support from its bureaucratic, public, and foreign environments. Drawing on the experiences of the five governments, I will first examine the patterns of highway bureaucracy performance and then housing bureaucratic performance.

HIGHWAYS: PROVIDING FOR THE ECONOMY

Public demand for highway infrastructure came late to Central America. Only since World War II has a concerted effort been made by the Central American governments to construct national and regional road networks. The delay in highway development is, in part, a product of the rate and form of the region's economic development. Since the late nineteenth century bananas and coffee have dominated the Central American economies and tied them primarily to foreign markets. Bananas, a product cultivated almost exclusively by foreign companies, were grown in coastal lowland regions and transported to nearby ports by company-owned railroads. Coffee, in contrast, was grown by natives in highland areas. The transportation of coffee, however, became the responsibility of the foreign-owned railroads that were built around the turn of the century.

Until 1940, then, the very specialized and limited transportation needs of the five countries were satisfied by railroads that connected agricultural regions with coastal ports. Not until World War II was there a concerted effort to link the five countries with each other. The initiative came, as it often has, from outside the region. The United States government, intent on securing a land route to the Panama Canal for defense purposes, offered to construct an all-weather road traversing the western highlands of Central America connecting Mexico with Panama. The impoverished Central American governments quickly accepted this development windfall.

With the Inter-American Highway project came American engineers, technicians, and contractors. Appalled by their discovery of the unprepared and ill-equipped highway agencies of the five countries, the Americans, led by the United States Bureau of Public Roads, immediately began training and equipping the local highway departments to maintain and administer the road system the North Americans were constructing.[2] The basic struc-

2. Typical of highway agency conditions in the late 1940s and early 1950s are those described by the Costa Rican Public Works Minister

tures of the region's highway department reflect these initial North American efforts.[3] To be sure, the Americans failed to resolve most of the technical, organizational, and managerial problems that plagued the Central American governments, but they did manage to create skeletal organizational structures and propose objectives toward which the governments could work in preparing for the developmental task that lay ahead.[4]

By the early 1950s the economic benefits of the Inter-American Highway had revealed the rewards of infrastructure development to Central American leaders. Coinciding with their

who, upon taking office, observed: "upon initiating our work in the Ministry we found a chaotic situation in the management of all ministerial equipment. . . . completing the chaotic spectacle were broken-down vehicles, half destroyed and abandoned construction equipment that was scattered in pieces blocking traffic in the streets surrounding the Ministry" (Ministerio de Obras Públicas, *Memoria 1954* [San José, 1965], p. 5).

3. While there were slight variations in the highway agency structures among the five governments, they generally adhered to the same basic design. Each highway department was the largest agency within the Ministry of Public Works and was composed of such departments as Planning, Administration, Design, Construction, Maintenance, and Shops. See TSC Consortium, *Central American Transportation Study* (Washington, 1965).

4. The impact of the Bureau of Public Roads in each country varied according to the degree of local receptivity and the volume of work required on the Inter-American Highway. It was deeply involved in Costa Rica and Nicaragua. In the former the Bureau's eighteen-man staff was not reduced substantially until the mid-1960s. Nicaragua's Somoza, as always, welcomed the Americans; because the offer of American assistance coincided with his desire to expand agricultural production through infrastructure development, he assigned them the task of organizing and equipping the Nicaraguan highway agency in 1950. In El Salvador and Guatemala, in contrast, the role of the Bureau of Public Roads was small, in the former because of the country's small size and in the latter because of occasional nationalistic resistance to foreign intrusion. Honduras, as usual, suffered from neglect. Since the Inter-American Highway traversed only the tip of southern Honduras, the Americans expressed little interest in its administrative development. See Republic of Costa Rica—United States Bureau of Public Roads, "Inter-American Highway Monthly Report" (June 1968), and República de Nicaragua, Ministerio de Fomento y Obras Públicas, Departamento de Carreteras, *Diez años al servicio de la patria 1955–1965* (Managua, 1966).

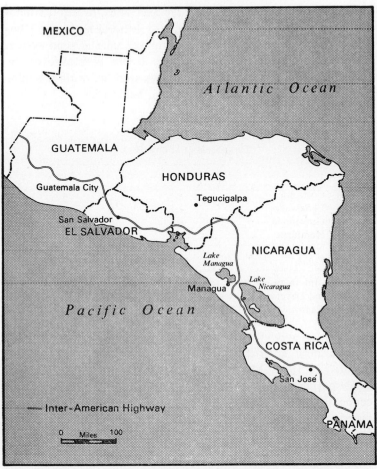

University of Wisconsin Cartographic Laboratory

MAP 1   Central American States.

awareness were the rise of indigenous development ideologies and new offers of foreign assistance. In 1950 the International Bank of Reconstruction and Development began supplying low interest loans to assist in the construction of national highway networks throughout the isthmus. On the recommendation of IBRD research teams highway construction became the principal target of IBRD assistance to the region.[5] Thus, by 1960 Guatemala's Atlantic Highway, El Salvador's Littoral Highway, Honduras' Western Highway, and Nicaragua's coastal road system were nearing completion, largely due to the assistance of the IBRD. And by 1965 the region's roads were more than double the length they had been in 1953. (See Table 15.)

TABLE 15
Paved and All-Weather Roads
(Thousands of kilometers)

	1953	1965
Costa Rica	1.8	4.8
El Salvador	1.5	4.3
Guatemala	4.4	7.6
Honduras	1.6	2.7
Nicaragua	1.0	3.1
Total	*10.3*	*22.5*

Source: International Bank for Reconstruction and Development, and International Development Association, *Economic Development and Prospects for Central America*, 7 vols. (Washington, 1967), 6:3.

The third, and most recent, stimulant to highway development is the Central American regional economic integration program initiated in 1958. The Inter-American Highway, essentially a single-purpose defense highway that aided the Central American economies only incidentally, was inadequate in meeting the demands of regional integration. Beginning in the late 1950s, therefore, United Nations technicians designed a thirteen-road regional network that was approved in 1963 by the five governments. During the late 1960s the Central American Bank for Economic Integration (CABEI) allocated approximately $113 million to the five governments to implement the regional highway program. Much of the burden of this program fell on Honduras which was selected as a priority area for regional highway development because of its underdeveloped infrastructure and central location in

5. See, for example, IBRD, *The Economic Development of Guatemala* (Baltimore: Johns Hopkins University Press, 1952) and IBRD, *The Economic Development of Nicaragua* (Baltimore: Johns Hopkins University Press, 1953).

the isthmus. It was assigned eight roads totaling 831 kilometers, compared to an average of only 92 kilometers of regional roads in each of the other four countries.[6]

Highway investments have taken a high priority in Central American development schemes, and in all countries except El Salvador highway construction has been the largest item in annual development budgets since 1964.[7] With the growth of regional integration in the mid-1960s has come renewed emphasis on highway infrastructure as a concommitant of regional development. Consequently, international agencies have continued their strong support of highway investments with loans and grants throughout the decade.

The performance of the highway departments of the Central American governments has been crucial to the region's development thrust. In two decades their budgets have expanded at least sixfold and their personnel more than doubled. At the same time, they have been forced, often reluctantly, to adjust their behavior to meet those growing demands. Administrative analysis, foreign advice, and self-criticism have been abundant as national planning agencies, regional and international agencies, and presidents have attempted to guide them through this difficult transition.

Reorganization: A Defensive Response

Structural reorganization has been one of the principal means of adjusting to demands for increased program execution. The appeal of reorganization is obvious: formal organization structures are identifiable and, on organization charts at least, amenable to change. There also exists a large body of organization and methods doctrine upon which the reorganizer can draw for guidance. In addition, the Central American highway departments have been encouraged and assisted with reorganization by the Central American School of Public Administration, a United Nations-supported regional training institution located in San

6. SIECA, *Informe preliminar: programa regional de carreteras centroamericanas*, vol. 1 (Guatemala, 1963).

7. See SIECA, Mision Conjunta de Programación para Centroamerica, *Resumen de los programas centroamericanos de inversiones públicas* (Guatemala, 1965).

José, Costa Rica.[8] In 1961, 1964, and 1965 ESAPAC held conferences for Central American highway administrators to discuss mutual organizational problems and propose common solutions. At the 1961 conference the delegates expressed general discontent with their performance and agreed upon forty recommendations for administrative improvement. Typical of these were suggestions for improvements in training, increased applications of civil service systems, greater use of cost/benefit analysis, more efficient budgetary procedures, and better management of foreign assistance.[9]

The regional meetings equipped highway administrators with reorganization doctrines. These new ideas, however, were catalysts to, not causes of administrative reorganization. The principal cause was dissatisfaction with highway agency management of highway projects in the early 1960s. With the increase in the number of projects had come delays in project execution, unanticipated project costs, and embarrassing technical errors. With doctrine in hand, highway administrators responded by offering reorganization as a means of coping with their management problems.

In reviewing the reorganization efforts of the decade, two patterns emerge from a comparison of the five governments: early in the decade reorganization was used to cope with program expansion; later in the decade it became a means of adjusting to program failures. During the first period the initiative and leadership were primarily external. Foreign assistance was offered to expand road construction and foreign consultants recommended the addition of new departments and additional staff to manage these programs because of their lack of confidence in the capacity

8. The Central American School of Public Administration (ESAPAC), now called the Central American Institute of Public Administration (ICAP), was created by a regional agreement in 1954 and has been advised and financed by the United Nations. Its principal functions include hosting conferences for administrators from the Central American governments and the instruction of administrators through short, specialized organization and methods courses. By 1968, 790 administrators had participated in conferences and 1,586 had received some form of instruction.

9. ESAPAC, *Informe del seminario sobre organización y administración de carreteras*, Tomo I (San José, 1961).

of the highway departments. Ideally, these initial reorganization measures would have been sufficient to cope with program expansion. In fact, they were not. By the mid-1960s numerous program failures, caused primarily by budgetary constraints and personnel problems, led to widespread criticism of highway department performance and the second phase of reorganization. The budgetary and personnel constraints, unfortunately, were inalterable; but, organization structures, in contrast, appeared amenable to change. International agencies, embarrassed presidents, and frustrated planning agency directors joined in demanding reorganization as a means of improving program execution. Consequently, ministers were changed, new programming units were added, and new departments created. In this way reorganization became the principal response to performance failures. Originally an instrument used to prevent performance problems, it became a means of coping with rising external and internal pressure on actual performance shortcomings. These patterns are most clearly revealed in the Costa Rican, Nicaraguan, and Honduran cases.

More than any other government in Central America, the Costa Ricans have responded to the pains of change by concentrating on the structural reorganization of their highway agency. As if guided by the belief that structural reorganization alone would solve the many problems that have plagued Costa Rican highway administration, Costa Rican officials have undauntedly followed the reorganization path. Participation by highway agency officials in the 1961 ESAPAC conference on highway administration heightened their awareness of discrepancies between their actual organizational structure and that which was needed to manage new highway programs. Using the recommendations of the meeting as a starting point, a ministerial official prepared a reorganization plan in 1962 proposing implementation of the recommendations of the regional meeting and the application of the "scientific principles of administration" advocated by F. W. Taylor and L. Urwick.[10] In October 1962 the

10. Enrique Soto Borbón, *Proposición para reorganizar el Ministerio de Obras Públicas* (San José, 1962).

Organization and Methods Office of the Finance Ministry completed a comprehensive study suggesting clearer lines of authority under the Highway Director through the use of five functional directorates.[11]

Despite the message of urgency contained in these recommendations, they were not implemented. In 1962 Ministry of Public Works officials were concerned with a different form of reorganization: the creation of a Ministry of Transportation. The Orlich administration, recognizing the growing problems of transportation policy coordination, sought to integrate all transportation policy-making within one ministry instead of three, as was the case in 1962. These efforts led to the conversion of the Public Works Ministry into the Ministry of Transportation in 1963.[12]

The second phase of Costa Rican highway reorganization began in mid-1966 after the inauguration of President José Trejos. Under pressure to improve implementation of the lagging National Highway Program, Trejos decided to remove some of the career highway agency officials whom he blamed for program failures. To both legitimize his decision and blunt opposition protest, Trejos asked the OFIPLAN Efficiency and Productivity Office to make a complete study of organization structures and propose a comprehensive reorganization scheme justifying the removal of several officials. When completed, however, the final study, largely because of the influence of Ministry of Transportation officials on the OFIPLAN team, rejected Trejos' demands for personnel changes.[13]

11. República de Costa Rica, Ministerio de Economía y Hacienda, Oficina de Organización y Métodos, *Proyecto para reorganizar el Ministerio de Obras Públicas* (San José, 1962).

12. República de Costa Rica, Ley Num. 3155, 5 agosto 1963. The law transferred the Educational Architecture Department (school construction) to the Ministry of Education and added the General Direction of Civil Aviation and the General Direction of Automotive Transport to the new Ministry of Transportation.

13. República de Costa Rica, OFIPLAN, Departamento de Productividad y Eficiencia Administrativa, *Ministerio de Transportes: Reorganización administrativa* (San José, 1968). OFIPLAN attempted a new strategy in implementing this study; instead of imposing the reforms from the planning agency, they coopted key Ministry of Transportation

The Nicaraguans resorted to structural reorganization less frequently than the Costa Ricans, but, when used, it was applied decisively. Their initial response to program expansion in the early 1960s differs greatly from that of Costa Rica. Where the Costa Ricans were suddenly thrust into major programs by their commitment to the large National Highway Program, the Nicaraguans benefitted from the gradual implementation of two World Bank projects in the late 1950s and an International Cooperation Administration/Agency for International Development supported project in the early 1960s. Also in contrast to Costa Rica, financial support by Nicaraguan presidents was more consistent and centralized governmental reorganization less frequent. Yet, the most striking difference between the two organization responses was the changes imposed by presidential fiat on the Nicaraguan highway agency during the fiscal crisis of 1968.

During its first phase of reorganization in the early 1960s the Nicaraguans added a new department to manage farm-to-market road projects and hired more engineers to supervise new loan programs signed with the Inter-American Development Bank. But this pattern of gradual organizational adjustment to program expansion was upset during the fiscal crisis of 1968. The highway agency, to everyone's surprise, became the principal victim of Somoza's austerity program. In May 1968 he dismissed 1000 of the agency's employees to reduce operating costs. This was followed by drastic reductions in national counterpart funds for foreign loans. But Somoza did not stop there. Later in 1968 he abolished the highway agency's Projects and Studies Division which included a staff of eight engineers and 150 technicians who had been trained over a fifteen-year period. This unexpected presidential behavior is explained in part by Somoza's dissatisfaction with increasing program execution problems and foreign pressures to resolve them during a time of fiscal crisis. It also results from Somoza's belief that the agency's project design operations could be performed more economically by private con-

---

personnel to conduct the study. In the end, the strategy led to the formal adoption of the reforms but it also reduced presidential control over the content of the reforms.

sultants. Throughout the year that followed Somoza boasted of his decision at political rallies throughout the country. In one speech he explained: "You know that last year I eliminated the highway agency's Projects and Studies Division because it consumed 4 million cordobas a year and didn't produce 400,000 cordobas. One of the principal beneficiaries of my removal of these lazy technicians is your province where we will build roads using the savings I have made."[14]

More than the other Central American countries, Honduras has been under intense foreign pressure to reshape its antiquated administrative structures. In the mid-1950s World Bank highway loans were made contingent on the implementation of reorganization schemes recommended by American consultants. The consultants reported in 1957 that the highway agency was primarily a one-man organization, that equipment was run down, and that too few skilled personnel were employed by the agency. With the aid of the consultants, the agency was reorganized, new statistics and personnel departments were created, and a new accounting and budget system was introduced.[15]

Despite these efforts and the continual assistance of foreign consultants during the early 1960s, the Honduran highway agency was plagued by more execution problems than any of the other Central American highway agencies. As development plan implementation stagnated in the mid-1960s the attention of international agencies, planning officials, and, ultimately, President López himself, focused on the highway agency's failure to implement the largest item in the development budget. In the fall of 1967, after intensive foreign and national criticism, President López finally committed himself to the reorganization of the agency. He first appointed Francisco Prats, a young architect who had distinguished himself as the able director of the national housing agency, as his new Minister of Public Works. Upon taking office Prats invited an organization and methods specialist

14. Quoted from the Nicaraguan daily newspaper, *Novedades*, 8 setiembre 1969, p. 11.

15. Republic of Honduras—Upham, Porter, Urquhart Associates, "Progress Report on Honduran Highway Maintenance Project, January 1956 to April 1957," mimeographed (Tegucigalpa, 1957), pp. 1–38.

from the Central American School of Public Administration to propose a reorganization scheme.

The reorganization proposal, completed in August 1968, identified the familiar personnel and procedural problems as the most serious obstacles to program implementation. It recommended a complete "structural reorganization" and the addition of ninety skilled employees.[16] These recommendations differed little from those that had flooded Honduras in the late 1950s and, like their predecessors, they were not implemented because of the lack of qualified personnel to fill new positions and supervise the scheme's implementation.

Of the five countries under examination, two do not conform to the two phase pattern described above. Both El Salvador and Guatemala are, to some extent, deviant cases. They differ primarily because each lacked conditions present in the other three cases: the absence of large highway programs in the Salvadorian case and the absence of vulnerability to external criticism in the Guatemalan case.

El Salvador, whose highway programs were a minor part of the national development plan, was subject to few pressures for reorganization. By 1960 El Salvador, having completed most of its national highway system, had turned to other development tasks. When its highway agency experienced execution problems in the mid-1960s they were minor and caused very little concern among international agencies and little embarrassment to the president. Without strong dissatisfaction and consequent pressures, highway agency officials were not compelled to initiate dramatic changes to impress critics.

Guatemala, in contrast, was pressured to eliminate program execution failures, but Guatemalan officials, because of a strong nationalistic tradition and lingering resentment of foreign technicians, proudly defied the demands of international agencies. Guatemala's size, historical dominance over Central America, and recent revolutionary experience have contributed to a sense of national pride that frequently produced firm reactions to for-

16. ICAP, *Informe sobre la organización y funcionamiento de la Dirección General de Caminos de Honduras* (San José, 1968).

eign demands. Their behavior during the two reorganization phases is illustrative of this pride and hostility.

As it did in Honduras, the World Bank in the late 1950s required reorganization of the highway agency as a precondition for a highway loan to Guatemala. Under the direction of American consultants the agency was reorganized in 1957. With foreign assistance, the foundation of an efficient highway agency was quickly created. Or so it appeared. Four months after the consultants departed the Guatemalans reorganized the agency nullifying nearly all of the changes made by the consultants.[17] The Guatemalans had resented the foreign-imposed changes. They also found them impractical. Foreign technicians, impressed by labor-saving technology, insisted on the use of modern equipment. The Guatemalans, seeking the incorporation of the largest possible rural labor force into the maintenance program, purposely tried to keep the use of heavy equipment to a minimum.

The conflict between Guatemalans and foreigners over reorganization continued during the second phase in the mid-1960s. The Bureau of Public Roads in 1964 conducted a thorough study, focussing on highway maintenance organization, in preparation for an Export-Import Bank highway maintenance loan. The study's recommendations differed little from those of the 1957 study. Equipment was inadequate, central control was lacking, and personnel were unqualified. There was need for training programs, a clean-up of shops filled with useless junk, new equipment, and the appointment of qualified section chiefs.[18] The 1964 reorganization proposal, however, was no more successful than that of 1957, for the Guatemalans simply refused to implement it. Initially they signed the Export-Import Bank loan and agreed to its conditions, which included the reorganization scheme, but the loan was never disbursed. Aware of bureaucratic opposition,

17. República de Guatemala, Ministerio de Obras Públicas y Comunicaciones, "Guatemalan Road Maintenance May 1955 to May 1959; Final Report of TAMS," mimeographed (Guatemala, 1969), p. 32.

18. USAID, "Guatemala: Highway Construction and Maintenance . . .," A Report Prepared by Paul Tysinger of the Bureau of Public Roads (May 24, 1964).

President Méndez killed the loan by refusing to appropriate counterpart funds.

Our comparison of the two phases of highway agency reorganization in the five Central American countries reveals a dominant pattern, one that is reinforced by the deviant cases. Large highway programs, strong foreign pressures, and domestic, particularly presidential, embarrassment over possible or actual program failures led to structural reorganization. The greater the importance of highway program implementation to the success of the national development plan, the greater were the pressures for action. Interestingly, highway agency officials used reorganization primarily to placate critics of agency performance. That is, it was a means of coping with the national planners and international agencies that were critical of the "mismanagement" of loans and grants to highway projects and insisted on reorganization as a means of improving management. To support compliance with these demands the international agencies offered technical assistance and made reorganization a condition of loan disbursement. Under such pressures, reorganization schemes became the highway administrator's most viable means of sustaining his desperately needed foreign financial support.

Structural Dualism: The Vicious Circle

Reorganization is one response to program execution shortcomings; foreign technical assistance is another. The justification for such assistance is simple: if the national bureaucracy cannot do the job, foreign technicians can. In Central America private foreign consultant firms assumed this role, usually at the request of the international agencies. The extent of required consultant services depended on the international agencies' estimate of the technical capacity of each highway agency. The minimum services included only the supervision of highway construction; the most extensive added feasibility studies and highway designing prior to construction.

The external demand for consultant services has aroused in recent years intense conflicts over strategies of administrative and technical learning throughout Latin America. The international agencies argue that in order to attain the objective of rapid project completion they must employ expert consultant services.[19] Others, particularly the national highway agencies, respond that continual reliance on consultants, while productive in the short-run, obstructs the development of local technical capacity. To many Central American highway agency officials the consultants became administrative colonialists intent on making their profit and satisfying the international agencies, but disinterested in the development of local competence.

Despite efforts to avoid dependence on foreign consultants, some Central American highway agencies became victims of the "administrative colonialism" and the growth of dual administrative structures. Comparative analysis of highway agency dependence on consultants reveals the degree of structural duality in the five highway agencies. Using consultant costs as a proportion of total construction costs as an indicator of dependence, a cross-national comparison is made in Table 16. The sample includes

TABLE 16
Consultant Costs as a Percentage of Construction Costs

Costa Rica	2.5
El Salvador	11.2
Guatemala	4.4
Honduras	12.9
Nicaragua	2.4
Average	*7.5*

Source: Banco Centroamericano de Integración Económica, *Análisis sobre servicios de ingenería para proyectos de factibilidad y de inversión en centroamerica financiados por el BCIE* (Tegucigalpa, 1968), p. 2.

all projects financed by the Central American Bank of Economic Integration between 1963 and 1968.[20] The data reveal significant variation in the degree of dependence among the five countries;

19. For the IBRD's justification of consultant services see John A. King, *Economic Development Projects and Their Appraisal: Cases and Principles from the Experience of the World Bank* (Baltimore: Johns Hopkins University Press, 1967), p. 8.

20. The difference in consultant costs is not the product of variations in fees, for the same rates were used by consultants in all of the countries.

dependence is high in Honduras and El Salvador, but, in contrast, is very low in Costa Rica, Nicaragua, and Guatemala.

One condition accounts for much of this variation: the role of the United States Bureau of Public Roads in the 1950s. The Costa Rican, Nicaraguan, and Guatemalan highway agencies were dominated by the Bureau in the 1940s and 1950s, while the others were not. In addition to its role as a consultant on the Inter-American Highway, the Bureau, a nonprofit public agency, sought to develop local engineering capabilities and phase out its own participation. By the mid-1960s the Bureau had left behind native engineering staffs that required only minimum assistance from foreign consultants.

In El Salvador, where the Inter-American Highway was completed quickly in the late 1940s, and in Honduras, where very little construction was necessary, the Bureau did not offer comparable training. Instead, both countries were forced by World Bank loans in the late 1950s to draw upon a wide range of services from foreign consultants. In fact, in each country one consultant firm dominated its highway agency from 1958 until 1966, designing all roads and supervising all construction. In effect, the agencies were transformed into maintenance organizations, abdicating their other functions to foreigners.

El Salvador and Honduras, because of their initial use of consultants, were caught in a vicious circle of administrative dependence and structural duality. The dilemma was aptly stated in the 1968 Honduran reorganization proposal: "What has happened in Honduras is that the consultant firms have taken on increasing functions to the detriment of the highway organization. It has reached the extreme where a consultant firm now delivers studies directly to the Minister without submitting them for analysis and approval by the Director of Highways. The situation has generated a vicious circle: the lack of confidence of the financial agencies and the increasing intervention of the consultants has weakened the self-confidence and technical capacity of the agency."[21]

By the end of the decade, Central American officials, particu-

21. ICAP, *Informe sobre . . . Honduras,* p. 10.

larly Hondurans and Salvadorians, who were once reluctant to question the demands of the international agencies, were loudly criticizing the dualistic structures that had been imposed on them. Their rising protest resulted from their frustration with foreign critics who, on the one hand, complained of poor administrative performance, but, on the other, supported managerial strategies that obstructed the development of local managerial and technical competence.

As the protests of the Central American governments increase, the international agencies are faced with a new dilemma. They must seek to assure the achievement of the objectives for which they loan money; however, in the long run, they too desire to increase the administrative capacity of national agencies. Unless they can use consultants to accomplish both objectives, as was skillfully done by the Bureau of Public Roads in the 1950s, they will have to sacrifice either their short- or their long-range goals.

The Human Resources Gap

Reorganization attacked structures, but it failed to eliminate operational problems. As we have seen, reorganization was, to a large extent, a means of satisfying complaints about operational problems that were not amenable to rapid change. As program failures increased and complaints rose, reorganization, not better-trained personnel, higher salaries, and expanded budgets, was offered as the remedy for performance problems.

The intransigence of operational obstacles was common to all Central American governments during the Development Decade. To be sure, there was some variation in the appearance and timing of the problems. In some, like Honduras, personnel problems were greater than financial, while in others, like Costa Rica and Guatemala, financial problems were dominant. Nevertheless, all experienced difficulties in adequately staffing their agencies and financing their operations during the period of expanding programs. To understand operational difficulties an analysis of their causes and effects is required; their causes are examined in the section that follows and their effects in the discussion of project behavior in Chapter 6.

Operating problems result from inadequate responses to program expansion. In the late 1950s and early 1960s Central American presidents rapidly expanded their national highway programs with the aid of foreign assistance. Such growth placed obvious new demands on their small highway agencies. Increased construction required additional engineers to design and supervise projects; expanded operations required more budgetary support; and new highway projects increased maintenance operations. Unfortunately, Central American presidents were more effective in initiating new programs than in expanding support for their management. Constrained by fluctuating fiscal conditions, scarce human resources, and their own preference for investment over operations, they gave very erratic replies to their planners' and administrators' pleas for increased support. This dissynchronization of program demands and presidential support is revealed most clearly in the areas of personnel, budgetary, and maintenance operations.

The success or failure of any program depends, in part, on the ability of the people who plan, organize, and carry out its numerous activities. In the Central American bureaucracies there is a scarcity of such qualified personnel. The problem lies in making public service careers attractive and rewarding to skilled personnel, particularly economists, accountants, and engineers, who are needed in government agencies. Recruitment problems are particularly acute in the more technical ministries, like public works. It has been observed, for example, that: "the present Highway Departments do not have enough men of long experience in highway engineering. Too many and too frequent changes in the administrative heads and in the department chiefs adversely effect efficient management . . . promotion within the departments has not been firmly placed on a merit system that impersonally evaluates the service records and capabilities of available personnel. This generates a feeling of a dissatisfaction in subordinate ranks and a high turnover in personnel."[22]

Civil service systems have been offered by the planners and international agencies as remedies for these personnel problems,

22. TSC Consortium, *Central American Highway Study*, vol. I (Washington, 1965), pp. 185–86.

but their application has been quite superficial. Even Costa Rica's merit system, which is the most complete in the region, applies to only a few of the highway agency personnel. These reforms failed because they clashed with presidential patronage powers. In all countries presidential patronage is an important political resource; in some, particularly Honduras and El Salvador, it is a crucial resource. The initiation of new highway programs brings a new conflict for presidential resolution. On the one hand, they must satisfy the demands of those political followers who desire administrative positions, but on the other, they must respond to demands, principally those of their own planning offices and the international agencies, for high quality agency staffing.

There are two general types of highway agency personnel—permanent and day labor. The former are the skilled, year-long employees; the latter, usually unskilled, are hired temporarily to work on particular maintenance and construction projects. Highway administrators are besieged by demands for day labor positions and have, as we saw in the Guatemalan case, resisted foreign efforts to introduce labor-saving machinery that might eliminate this opportunity to distribute jobs. The continuation of patronage to day laborers would have little ill effect on performance, but the opposite is true of skilled positions where the elimination of patronage is essential to better performance. Central American presidents, because of their obsession with the acquisition of political support, have failed to distinguish between the relative costs and benefits of the two distinct uses of their patronage powers and have allowed political considerations to dominate all government hiring.

Even if patronage were eliminated, there remain other problems in attracting skilled personnel to the highway agencies. There are several disadvantages to working for a public agency in these countries, the most common of which is the very low salaries.[23] The Nicaraguan administrators, moreover, have added

23. Costa Rican administrators complained that: "there have been difficulties in recruiting and keeping technical and specialized personnel because the salaries paid by the Central Government ministries are low in comparison with private enterprises and autonomous institutes." The Hondurans similarly complained that: "the principal causes of this situa-

their own variation of the salary problem. While they are reluctant to discuss it, they complain that they are required to contribute 2 percent of their already low salaries to the Somozas' National Liberal party; failure to do so, they add, leads to immediate dismissal.

Personnel problems, like others in the chain of policy implementation, cannot be isolated from the larger political process of each nation. They are products of presidential use of patronage, the distribution of scarce budgetary resources, the competitiveness of the public and private sectors, and educational opportunities. If the presidents of Central American countries continue to be constrained by their scarce and fluctuating resources and constant demands for political patronage, their public agency personnel problems will persist in hindering development program performance.

Funding: The Price of Performance

Of all of the highway agencies' travails, those associated with funding have been the most serious impediments to smooth operations. For although budgetary allocations to the agencies have increased, they have fallen far short of the needs of expanding agency operations. At the urging of their planners Central American presidents accepted foreign loans to cope with their financial resource shortages, but, to their displeasure, such assistance did not solve their problem. Foreign loans demanded the allocation of more, not less, national resources through their matching fund requirements; as a result, Central American presidents increased rather than relieved their financial problems. The constraints imposed on agency operations by financial shortcomings are revealed by an examination of budgetary procedures and levels of national and foreign financing.

Procedural controls have plagued Central American adminis-

---

tion [the lack of trained personnel] are: the lack of vocational schools, the instability of employment, the delays in salary payments because of excessive paperwork in the payroll office." See ICAP, *Informe de la primera reunion de Directores Generales de Caminos del Istmo Centroamericano* (San José, 1967), pp. 29, 126.

tration since the establishment of Spanish rule over the region. The rigidity and detail of the Spaniards' formal bureaucratic regulations increased with one's distance from the Crown. In practice, much of this detailed regulation was ignored at the local level in response to local conditions. Yet, despite its frequent irrelevance, bureaucratic formalism survived independence and lingers as one of the strongest Spanish legacies throughout the isthmus. Formal surveillance over detailed administrative operations is the guiding principle of Central American public administration. As a result, a complex system of elaborate, but exceedingly inefficient, controls circumscribe all administrative operations.

The system is tolerated by Central American presidents despite its obvious inefficiency. They have given little support to the reorganization schemes of planners and foreign advisors who have tried to "liberate" their administrative systems of these cumbersome controls. Presidents acted, however, not in ignorance but with full recognition of the political costs of reorganization schemes. For them bureaucratic formalism is not just an obstacle to improved operations, but an opportunity for political support. Their formalistic bureaucratic structures guarantee extensive patronage opportunities for their semi-skilled supporters, for they offer hundreds of tasks, most requiring the performance of simple functions, that can be distributed as rewards for political support. To terminate this source of patronage, even for the desirable objective of improved performance, presidents would have to relinquish one of their important political resources.[24]

The management of public funds is the most formalistically controlled of all bureaucratic operations. The logic of the budgetary process is quite simple: in a system where no one can be trusted, everyone must participate. As a result, money is allocated in small amounts, for short periods, and must gain the approval of numerous officials before reaching its destination. Agency operational flexibility, a minor concern of those who direct the system,

24. This and the other analyses of patronage in the text are based largely on interviews with public officials; see Note on Sources.

is often lost under the rigorous enforcement of the network of controls.

In Honduras, one of the most patronage-ridden systems, budgetary rigidity frustrated and circumscribed highway agency operations. One official complained that: "the principal cause of delays in operations of the highway department is an administrative system excessively complicated by so many controls. In addition, the rigidity of the budget procedure that forces all decisions to wait for approval by the budget officer for routine financial decisions adds to the delays."[25] The Honduran budget office, located in the Ministry of Finance, controls expenditures through monthly allotments to the highway agency. Its rigid procedures, however, prevent budgetary adjustment to the highway agency's financial needs during peak periods of construction and maintenance activity. In addition, cumbersome auditing and procurement operations also prevent flexible and rapid agency operations. One recent study, for example, estimated that a highway agency purchase order had to pass through seventy-two people before the procurement activity was completed.[26]

Even in Costa Rica, where patronage is less pervasive than Honduras, bureaucratic formalism constrains agency operations. As in Honduras, funds are allocated on a monthly basis. In addition, the Treasury, in an effort to assure "fiscal responsibility," insists on a monthly balancing of expenditures and revenues; to assure success, the Treasury will often delay from one to six months funds due the Ministry of Transportation or private contractors. In many cases funds obligated by the Legislature to the Ministry are never disbursed because the Treasury fails to collect anticipated revenue during the fiscal year. Typical of such differences is the 1966 experience in which the legislature authorized 147.4 million *colones* to the Ministry, but the Treasury disbursed only 89.5 million.[27]

Despite constant pressures to over commit and under support programs, Central American presidents have managed to expand

25. Ibid., p. 128.
26. ICAP, *Informe sobre . . . Honduras*, p. 14.
27. Data supplied by OFIPLAN, the Costa Rican planning agency.

total budgetary support to their highway agencies during the Development Decade. In Table 17 highway agency expenditures

TABLE 17
Total Government and Highway Agency Expenditures Compared
(Millions of Dollars)

	Total Government		Highway Agency		Highway Agency as percent of Total Government	
	1961	1965	1961	1965	1961	1965
Costa Rica	61.2	83.5	3.0	8.0	5.0	10.0
El Salvador	68.9	99.9	8.7	9.9	12.6	10.0
Guatemala	105.1	166.9	11.2	17.6	10.6	10.5
Honduras	59.7	83.5	3.9	7.6	6.6	9.0
Nicaragua	39.2	66.5	3.9	15.3	9.8	23.0

Source: TSC Consortium, *Central American Transportation Study*, vol. 1 (Washington, 1965), p. 170.

(administrative, construction, and maintenance) in 1961 and 1965 are compared. Evident from these data is the dramatic expansion of expenditures in all countries but El Salvador, where investment programs were significantly reduced after 1961. Budgetary expansion was greatest in Costa Rica and Nicaragua both in absolute terms and as proportions of total public sector budgets. In Honduras and Guatemala, growth was, although not so spectacular, still quite significant. Nevertheless, these data, however impressive, tell only part of the story. If we move from the general to the particular, from the budgetary aggregate to the individual highway project, a very different conclusion emerges.

Central American presidents persistently failed to provide adequate financial support for their highway projects. Throughout the decade projects had to be delayed or reduced in size because anticipated levels of national funding, particularly in the matching of loans, were not attained. Examples abound. The Costa Rican National Road and Farm-to-Market Road Programs were cut back by President Orlich because of budgetary constraints. The Nicaraguan Plan Lechero suffered a similar fate at the hands of President Somoza as did El Salvador's National Road Program under President Sánchez. In each case, large parts of the project were eliminated because national financing was unavailable. These projects and several others will be examined in more detail in Chapter 6.

Another indicator of financial shortcomings is expenditures for maintenance operations. During the decade road construction and traffic volumes increased significantly. But, with the exception of Nicaragua, expenditure for highway maintenance did not keep pace with this expansion. During the 1959–64 period maintenance expenditures increased in El Salvador from $1.4 million to only $1.5 million, while in Guatemala they actually declined from $5.7 million to $5.6 million, and in Honduras from $3.5 million to $2.3 million.[28]

Presidential failure to allocate sufficient funds for highway maintenance was not always caused by lack of highway user revenues, as might be expected. For example, if we examine one case, such as El Salvador, we find that highway user-related revenues exceeded highway agency budgets. (See Table 18.) One

TABLE 18
El Salvador: Highway Budgets and Highway User Taxes Compared
(Millions of US $)

	1962	1963	1964	1965
Highway Taxes	10.0	10.7	11.2	14.0
Highway Budgets	6.7	6.4	8.7	9.9
Surplus	3.3	4.3	2.5	4.1

Sources: T S C Consortium, *Central American Transportation*, vol. 1 (Washington, 1965), p. 170; F. C. Meltzer, *Informe final sobre transportes* (San Salvador: Ministerio de Obras Públicas, 1967), p. 29.

might expect that with such surpluses Salvadorian presidents could easily meet maintenance budget requirements. Yet as we know, they have not done so. There are two explanations for this apparent incongruity. First, in El Salvador, as in the other four Central American countries, the earmarking of revenues for par-

28. SIECA, *Estudio sobre mantenimiento regional de carreteras centroamericanas* (Guatemala, 1966), p. 50.

ticular programs, so common in the United States, is constitutionally prohibited. Highway-related taxes must go into a general fund from which the president makes all of his budgetary allocations.[29] Second, Salvadorian presidents, again like their Central American counterparts, favor more spectacular new investments over less impressive maintenance operations. A recent survey of Central American maintenance operations concluded that: "unfortunately, highway maintenance, in contrast to highway construction, brings neither glory nor fame to those who undertake it. The opportunity to do something more visible and more praised by the public and the press is generally preferred. The bounty of maintenance operations is difficult to evaluate and the counter pressures of particular interests on highway officials are very strong."[30]

The substitution of new construction for maintenance is common in road-building in developing countries. Albert Hirschman, for example, has observed that different countries require different "mixes" of maintained and under-maintained mileage. More important, he notes, "up to a certain point the neglect of maintenance or the poor quality of roads so often noted in the developing countries is not just negligence and inertia, but a rational adaption to distinctive requirements of the economy."[31] Such transference of resources is unequivocally "bad" only when tampering with the quality of maintenance does not release resources that can be and are used to increase the quantity of new construction.[32]

We cannot measure the degree of "waste" in the construction-maintenance mixes of the Central American governments, but we can identify some common patterns of resource allocations to

29. While the prohibition on earmarking may contribute to financial inconstancy, its use might not guarantee adequate performance. Several observers have pointed out that financial sinecure also invites parasitism among administrative agencies. See, for example, Albert Hirschman, *Journeys Toward Progress* (New York: Anchor Books, 1965), pp. 50–58.

30. SIECA, *Estudio sobre mantenimiento regional*, Segundo Parte, Capitulo II.

31. Albert Hirschman, *Development Projects Observed* (Washington: The Brookings Institution, 1967), pp. 115–16.

32. Ibid., p. 113.

these two activities. Some poor maintenance was, by the highway administrators' own admission, the product of the theft of public funds. More common though was the use of maintenance equipment in response to local political demands for the construction of town squares, football fields, and municipal roads. Highway administrators also admit to another type of quantity-quality mix. Occasionally they sought to extend the length of road projects by lowering their quality. Although often rebuked by the foreign consultants who argued for high standards, the highway administrators maintained that the exchange of quality for quantity was a short-run necessity. They also admitted, however, that lower quality did not result only from the pursuit of greater quantity. Quite frequently, in fact, lower quality was not caused by stretching mileage but by the underestimation of construction costs and the consequent need to spread funds thinly to complete the road project.

Despite its burdensome impact on operations, foreign assistance greatly aided highway construction during the Development Decade. To a large extent Central Americans depended on foreign assistance for initiative and support during this period. During the 1961–65 period foreign assistance accounted for more than one-half of highway construction in two countries and over 40 percent in two others. (See Table 19.)

TABLE 19
Highway Construction Expenditures, 1961–1965

	Total[a]	Percentage Foreign Financed
Costa Rica	26	44
El Salvador	23	40
Guatemala	38	57
Honduras	31	62
Nicaragua	32	21

[a] In millions of dollars.

Source: International Bank for Reconstruction and Development, and International Development Association, *Economic Development and Prospects for Central America*, 7 vols. (Washington, 1967), 1:3.

Foreign financial assistance often rescued Central American development programs; but, as we have seen, it was a deceptive savior. Foreign assistance was destined primarily for new investments, not administration or maintenance. While appearing to support agency operations, it actually expanded them and increased agency budgetary demands. First, foreign loans had to be matched by local counterpart funds; second, operational expenditures had to be increased to manage new, more complex projects; and third, loans eventually had to be repaid. Thus, as investment budgets were rescued, operations budgets simultaneously became overburdened.

The Development Decade was a difficult time for the highway agencies of the Central American governments. Persistently they were the victims of excessive demands and insufficient support to meet those demands. They were criticized for their traditional structures, frequent program failures, and their resistance to change. At the same time, bureaucrats complained of inadequate presidential support and foreign understanding. They came to see themselves trapped by conditions over which they had little control and used as scapegoats by officials in their own governments who were unwilling or unable to alter those conditions.

PUBLIC HOUSING: PROVIDING FOR THE POOR

Until the late 1940s virtually all Central American housing had been accumulated through private initiative, determined by market forces together with the aspirations and savings capacity of individual families, and subject to only limited regulation by the state. But it became apparent by the late 1940s, largely through Pan American Union housing studies, that an urban housing problem existed throughout the region. The problem derived in part from population increase, rural to urban migration resulting from agricultural stagnation, and rising standards for evaluating the fitness of housing. In addition, public officials for the first time acknowledged that inflated land prices, costly and inefficient construction techniques, the high costs of credit, and the lack of effective legal protection and technical advice for families wishing to invest in housing dissuaded most middle and low income Central American families from saving for housing.[33]

One by one the Central American governments responded to their housing problem by creating autonomous housing agencies and initiating housing programs. To be sure, some feeble housing programs had been initiated in the area, particularly in El Salvador and Costa Rica, during the 1920s and 1930s; nevertheless, the creation of new agencies and programs in the early 1960s marked a distinct new departure for the public sector.[34]

To some extent the new housing programs were the products of the new wave of reformism that engulfed the region after 1945. Although housing policy was given only minor substantive importance, it became a symbol of regime commitment to the modern welfare values that were espoused during the period. El Salvador's military reformers, having just created their PRUD party, were the first to create an autonomous housing agency in 1950. They were soon followed by the Costa Ricans who, after making a national commitment to housing policy in their Consititution of 1949, created their own agency in 1953. The young Honduran junta that permitted the election of liberal Villeda Morales in 1957 initiated a housing program just before Villeda's inauguration. And finally, Nicaragua, as part of Luis Somoza's attempt to "liberalize" his regime after his father's death, created a housing agency in 1957. Modeled after Pan American Union proposals, all of the agencies shared structural similarities. All were semi-autonomous, were guaranteed an annual subsidy from the national budget, and with minor variations, consisted of such departments as Engineering, Programming, Finance, Administration, and Social Work. Their sizes ranged from 100 employees in Nicaragua to approximately 300 in El Salvador.

33. See United Nations Economic Commission for Latin America, "Social Development and Social Planning: A Survey of Conceptual and Practical Problems in Latin America," *Economic Bulletin for Latin America* 11 (April 1966): 53; Ruben Utria, "The Housing Problem in Latin America in Relation to Structural Development Factors," ibid. (October 1966): 81–110.

34. On Central American housing during the 1930s and 1940s see OEA, Union Panamericana, *La vivienda de interés social en América Latina* (Washington, 1957).

Guatemala was the only exception to this pattern, largely because of its peculiar "revolutionary" experience between 1944 and 1954. President Arevalo, intent on increasing the government's role in public housing, created a Department of Housing in his new Development Institute in 1948. His efforts, however, met with little success.[35] New housing program initiatives followed the election of President Arbenz in 1952, but he too failed to implement most of his proposals. It was not until Guatemala was overwhelmed by American assistance programs in 1956 that a housing agency was created. The agency, a product of a bilateral agreement, was ostensibly administered by Guatemalans, but actually was directed by five American International Cooperation Administration (ICA) technicians.[36]

The Pan American Union's public housing strategy appealed to the Central American presidents. Their new housing agencies offered additional sources of patronage, and public housing projects became highly visible symbols of presidential commitment to the urban lower class. In addition, presidents were convinced that their housing agencies could effectively deal with their national housing problems; the agencies could, in theory at least, buy large tracts of land at low cost, mobilize and modernize the national construction industry, and supply mass-produced, low-cost housing to the urban masses.

The presidents' initial optimism was not completely justified, however, for their housing agencies constructed very few houses during the 1950s. For example, El Salvador, the region's largest producer of public housing, constructed an annual average of 545 units between 1950 and 1959, while Costa Rica, the only other significant producer during the 1950s, constructed an annual average of 301 units between 1955 and 1960.[37]

35. Between 1948 and 1952 the Guatemalan Department of Housing constructed only 104 housing units for low income families.

36. República de Guatemala, Ministerio de Communicaciones y Obras Públicas, *El programa del Instituto Cooperativo Interamericana de la Vivienda* (Guatemala, 1960), pp. 29–44.

37. República de El Salvador, IVU, *Viviendas construidas por el instituto* (San Salvador, 1968) and República de Costa Rica, INVU, *Memoria 1966* (San José, 1966).

Central American presidents quite naturally looked to international agencies for assistance to expand their programs, but their pleas fell on deaf ears, for a "devil taking housing" theory prevailed among international agencies during the 1950s. According to this theory, housing merits low priority in national and international spending schemes because it is a durable form of investment requiring substantial outlays but paying off little per year. In addition, it generates no foreign exchange, competes with industry and agriculture for capital, draws off needed labor and materials, and many even be inflationary.[38]

The theory's dominance was broken, although only partially, by the initiation of the Alliance for Progress in 1961 and the emergence of the planners who sought to expand social infrastructure investment. The Alliance fostered the creation of the American financed Social Progress Trust Fund of the Inter-American Development Bank (IDB).[39] Through the Fund have flowed the principal loans for Central American public housing during the Development Decade. (See Table 20.)

Reorganization and Policy Coordination

Housing agency reorganization patterns differ substantially from those of the region's highway agencies. They were much fewer, of lesser consequence, and oriented toward policy consolidation rather than improved operations. Such immense differences merit some explanation.

Several conditions identified as causes of highway agency reorganization were not present in the housing policy arena. First, the expansion of programs after 1960 did not catch the housing agencies by surprise. Unlike the highway agencies, they were of recent creation and were designed, principally by foreign techni-

38. Charles Abrams, *Man's Struggle for Shelter in An Urbanizing World* (Cambridge, Mass.: MIT Press, 1964), p. 106.
39. The Social Progress Trust Fund is the product of an American effort to multilateralize aid to Latin America. Under an agreement of June 1961 the IDB administers a fund of $394 million supplied by the US government; in 1964 the US supplied an additional $131 million. These funds were allocated by the IDB as soft loans to the policy areas of agriculture, water supplies, housing, and education.

TABLE 20
Social Progress Trust Fund Housing Loans, 1960–1967

	Loan[a]	Total Proj. Cost.[a]	No. of Units
Costa Rica			
1961	$3.5	$16.0	5,725
1965	3.6	6.5	2,816
El Salvador			
1962	6.1	11.3	5,000
1965	6.0	11.1	4,415
Guatemala			
1962	5.3	10.7	5,795
Honduras			
1963	1.0	1.5	716
Nicaragua			
1962	5.1	7.8	2,910
1965	5.2	10.2	3,774
Total	*35.8*	*75.1*	*31,151*

[a] Figures in millions of dollars.

Source: International Development Bank, *Eighth Annual Report* (Washington, 1967), pp. 130–38.

cians, to manage programs the size of those financed by the IDB. Thus there was no demand for reorganization in preparation for the new programs as there had been in the highway agencies. Second, and perhaps more important, housing programs were very small items in national development programs. Consequently, when implementation problems occured in the national development plan, the planners' attention did not turn to housing programs, but centered, as we have seen, on such items as the large highway programs. Thus, because of their low visibility and their low priority, the housing agencies escaped similar foreign and domestic pressures to reorganize.

When housing reorganizations were attempted they came in response to less pressing concerns. Not long after their creation the autonomous housing agencies were joined in the housing policy arena by government-subsidized savings and loan and mortgage guarantee programs directed at middle and lower middle income groups. Soon thereafter central bank authorities, encouraged by the recommendations of international agencies, decided to impose some central coordination on their proliferating housing programs by merging existing housing agencies into one organization, usually taking the form of a national housing bank.

Despite strong foreign pressure, however, these reorganization schemes succeeded only in Nicaragua. There, with the assistance of USAID advisors, a National Housing Bank was created in 1966 combining a savings and loan division, a mortgage guarantee division, and the housing agency that Luis Somoza had created in 1957.[40] In El Salvador, in contrast, a National Housing Bank was created in 1965 but it remained separate from the public housing agency. Guatemala and Honduras represent the other extreme; in both countries the government failed altogether to implement USAID recommended savings and loan schemes. Given these diverse patterns, how does one explain the Nicaraguan success and the other failures? All of the countries were urged by USAID and the IDB to implement the housing bank reorganization schemes and each was offered technical assistance. Yet only one succeeded.

Two conditions emerge as factors which account for these differences. The success of the housing bank scheme is linked to the absence of opposition from the private banking community and the cooperation of the public housing agency. In Nicaragua there was little banking opposition and the housing agency fully cooperated. The Somozas exercised firm financial and personal control over the Nicaraguan banking system, including the foreign banks, and used the threat of governmental reprisal to discourage any opposition to their housing bank scheme. Housing agency officials also had little opportunity to mount an opposition. Since its creation, the agency had been closely tied to the Central Bank and had developed no real autonomy. Moreover, to remove their hesitancy about the scheme, housing agency officials were granted the directorships of the new housing bank.

In Guatemala and Honduras, in contrast, the banking community obstructed the creation of government-subsidized savings and loan institutions which they viewed as threats to their own savings and loan operations. In Guatemala the weak and vulner-

40. USAID, "Capital Assistance Paper: Nicaragua Housing and Savings and Loan System 1966," mimeographed.

able Méndez regime did not even bother to submit the necessary legislation after it learned of the bankers' opposition. In Honduras legislative proposals were submitted in 1964 under pressure from the IDB, but they were not enacted.[41] Finally, in 1967 international agencies made all housing loans to Honduras contingent on the creation of a savings and loan system and the law was finally passed. Yet, by the end of the decade the legislation still awaited implementation.

The Salvadorian pattern differs from both of the above because its housing bank scheme encountered resistance not from the banking community but from the public housing agency. As the oldest and largest housing agency in the region, the Salvadorian agency had developed significant autonomy and clientele support by the early 1960s. Exercising its influence, the agency succeeded in retaining its full autonomy when savings and loan institutions were created under a new housing bank in 1963. In addition, the agency has developed sufficient bureaucratic power to have resisted successive attempts by the IDB and the Salvadorian planning agency to alter its internal organization.[42]

Scarce Capital and Surplus Clientele

Two operational patterns, both related to financing, emerge from a comparison of the five Central American housing agencies. On the one hand, agency operations, despite substantial foreign assistance, were constrained by capital shortages and unreliable budgetary support; on the other, they were limited by a confused and unpredictable clientele.

Capital shortage is most apparent if the five national housing agencies are divided according to size, for capital shortages are closely associated with program size, i.e., the more ambitious the program beyond a minimum threshold, the greater the capital

41. OAS, Pan American Union, *Housing in Honduras* (Washington: Pan American Union, 1964), p. 41; República de Honduras, *Informe nacional del progreso económica y social de Honduras* (Tegucigalpa, 1966).

42. República de El Salvador, CONAPLAN, *Informe trimestral de proyectos de inversión pública al deciembre de 1966* (*San Salvador, 1967*), p. 26.

shortages. As expenditures for social infrastructure grow beyond a token level, they begin to compete with economic infrastructure expenditures for scarce budgetary resources. It was from this battle that the large housing programs emerged as losers. Only two countries, El Salvador and Costa Rica, passed beyond what might be termed a minimum threshold. In both countries budgetary subsidies of housing programs averaged more than 1 percent of the national budget, while in the other three countries subsidies were much less than 1 percent. As fiscal crisis struck the Central American countries in the mid-1960s, the three countries with small housing programs were able to sustain their small budgetary subsidies, but the Costa Rican and Salvadorian presidents were forced into hasty retreat from their original budgetary commitments. A review of each case is instructive.

The principal sources of financial support for the Costa Rican housing program, as in the other countries, were the budgetary subsidy, foreign loans, bond sales, payments on mortgages, and property income. Budgetary subsidies and payments on mortgages formed the core of this support. The Costa Rican housing agency was guaranteed 3 percent of the national budget until President Orlich, struggling to free himself from budgetary obligations, replaced the 3 percent subsidy with a smaller subsidy of 8 million *colones* after 1963. The 8-million level, while insufficient for dramatic program expansion, could have sustained existing operations if it were consistently maintained. But, unfortunately, it was not. Presidents Orlich and Trejos, forced to implement austerity measures, consistently reduced appropriations to the housing agency below the 8-million level. In fact, their actual subsidies were only 2.9 million, 3.9 million, and 4.7 million in 1964, 1965, 1966, respectively.[43] Subsidy reductions, as could be expected, had a disastrous impact on Costa Rican housing programs. Projects were reduced in size, personnel was dismissed, and, as will be seen in Chapter 6, project performance and loan implementation were seriously damaged.

The El Salvadorian budgetary subsidy to housing has been

43. República de Costa Rica, OFIPLAN, Departamento de Planes Anuales, *Informes 1965, 1966, 1967* (San José, 1966, 1967, 1968).

declining since the housing program's dramatic debut under President Osorio in 1950. Under Osorio the subsidy reached a peak of $4.1 million in 1953 but fell to an annual average of $1.8 million under Lemus in the late 1950s.[44] Again, between 1962 and 1966, the budgetary subsidy was reduced, this time to an annual average of $1 million; and in 1967, when President Sánchez encountered major fiscal problems, it was cut to $400,-000, producing a curtailment of agency operations. Witnessing their budgetary decline, housing agency officials demanded that they be guaranteed 3 percent of the national budget as had been done in Costa Rica before 1963.[45] Thus, ironically, as the Costa Rican president was freeing himself from similar budgetary obligations, the Salvadorian housing officials were trying to impose them on their president. They were, however, no more successful than their Costa Rican counterparts. President Sánchez, frantically searching for greater budgetary flexibility, ignored the agency's requests for a guaranteed subsidy.

Capital shortages cannot be properly understood without an awareness of the second operational pattern identified above: agency interaction with its unpredictable clientele. The lack of cooperation took many forms, but the most serious was the unwillingness or inability to make mortgage payments on houses. The housing agencies had planned their financial operations around the assumption of consistent returns on their investments. But because of inconsistent mortgage payment patterns by their clients, they were forced to operate within a financial straitjacket.

Housing programs were major innovations in Central American policy-making because they sought to pioneer new relationships between public institutions and the urban poor. The creation of these relationships, however, was strewn with numerous obstacles, not the least of which was a misunderstanding between agency officials and their clients. The agencies attempted to forge new formal bureaucratic and financial relationships with a sector of the population that had depended on traditional pa-

44. República de El Salvador, IVU, *Forma de financiamiento en los programas de viviendas de 1951 a 1967* (San Salvador, 1968)

45. República de El Salvador, CONAPLAN, *Plan de la Nación 1965–1969* (San Salvador, 1964), p. 568.

ternalistic relationships to satisfy its welfare needs. Politics and administration had been dominated by local leaders who acted as patrons in structuring the political and social life of the poor. Within this system, rewards, particularly public employment and physical protection, were provided in return for electoral or military support and labor. The use of new public institutions to supply benefits to the poor greatly altered this pattern. Bureaucratic rules, budgets, loans, and regular mortgage payments became components of this new welfare administration. Along with the institutionalization of the role of government have come expectations by reformist public officials that have not been shared by the lower class clientele. A major example of this incongruity has been the apparent unwillingness or inability of public housing recipients to pay their mortgages. They have come to expect benefits from government, but they have not accepted their new financial obligations. In the process they have weakened the housing agency's capability to realize its policy objectives.

The pattern of lagging mortgage payments is common to all five countries, although its impact was most severe in El Salvador and Costa Rica where large programs depended heavily on mortgage payments to support new investments. In 1967 the proportion of home purchasers who were at least three months delinquent in their payments ranged from the low of 38 percent in Honduras and El Salvador to a high of 70 percent and 75 percent in Costa Rica and Nicaragua, respectively.

The Inter-American Development Bank, quite naturally, viewed these conditions with alarm and demanded tighter enforcement of mortgage contracts as a condition of new housing loans after 1967. Remedial action by the housing agencies was complicated, however, by their clients' power of resistance. For example, after the IDB demanded tighter enforcement, the Salvadorian housing agency created a new payments collection section; but just as they began to implement firmer collection policies, the agency's clients mounted a vocal protest through the use of the nation's opposition political parties. The agency had announced that it would evict all clients who failed to pay all of their debts within fifteen days. Spokesmen for the opposition political parties seized the issue and denounced the government for callous treatment of the lower class that it had promised to serve. Shocked by the unexpected outbursts, the agency directors withdrew their demand for immediate mortgage payments.[46]

Confronted by capital shortages and constraints on mortgage recuperations, Central American presidents and their housing agency officials vigorously sought foreign assistance as a means of rescue. Foreign loans provided short-term solutions, for the IDB loan programs fit well into the schemes of the Central American housing agencies. The long-run problem of stable financial support, however, remained unsolved. The objectives of the IDB program were narrow and were based on the assumption that: "international assistance cannot substitute for measures which must originate in the countries themselves, such as those relating to income levels and distribution, employment and urban land reform, but it can provide seed capital and technical aid, and stimulate innovations in construction and financing."[47] By the end of the decade it was apparent that the Central American governments needed more than seed capital. The IDB loans had succeeded temporarily in inflating housing programs, but they left the housing agencies incapable of continuing them at the same rate. This was clearly revealed when the IDB announced in 1968 that it was terminating project loans for housing.[48] The housing agency directors panicked. In desperation they sent a joint memorandum to the IDB in Washington, D.C., pleading for the renewal of loan authorizations. In it they admitted for the first time that even "with the IDB loans and local subsidies, our agencies have not developed sufficient capital to permit a continuation of low cost housing programs."[49]

46. See the Salvadorian daily newspaper, *La Prensa Grafica* 3 febrero 1968.

47. IDB, *Social Progress Trust Fund Report, 1963* (Washington, 1964), p. 20.

48. The IDB did not completely withdraw from the housing field, but did reorient its program by including housing loans as small parts of large urban development loans. Because they were unable to develop large-scale urban development programs in a short time, the Central American housing agencies did not qualify under the new programs. In the short run then, they lost their principal source of funds.

49. Nicaragua, Instituto Nacional de Vivienda; Honduras, Instituto

Central American presidents were in part responsible for the long-run crises faced by their housing agencies. They had seized the IDB loans as a source of rescue, not as a stimulant to further institutional and program development. In most cases they reduced budgetary subsidies and depended entirely on the IDB loans for investment capital in order to release budgetary resources for higher priority policy objectives. To be sure, their policies produced several thousand houses for the urban poor; but it is equally apparent that their actions did not prepare their housing agencies for greater productivity in the decade ahead.

THE BUREAUCRATIC OBSTACLE

The examination of bureaucratic performance has revealed a few differences and many similarities between Central America's highway and housing agencies. The two bureaucracies were differentiated most clearly by the clienteles they served. Highway agency clients were dispersed geographically and socially and generally responded as participants in the market economy. Only infrequently did they involve themselves directly in agency operations. Highway administrators, consequently, responded primarily to presidential policy demands and the offerings of international agencies. In contrast, housing agencies, like most social welfare agencies, confronted a more concentrated clientele which had more direct impact on its operations. Client behavior is a crucial part of the output of a welfare agency and, as we have seen, can frequently operate as a constraint on agency performance. Unlike the highway agency, the housing agency's basic problem was not technical but behavioral and its principal instruments were not the simple transference of foreign technology and resources, but the adaptation of both to local conditions. Housing administrators sought not only to build new housing but also to reshape the life styles of low income families.

The two bureaucracies were also differentiated by the size of

---

Nacional de Vivienda; El Salvador, Instituto de Vivienda Urbana; Guatemela, Instituto Nacional de Vivienda, "Commentarios al documento GN–140–1 del Banco Interamericano de Desarrollo" (Letter to IDB, 1968).

their projects and their relative importance to the planners' development programs. As one of the largest items in the national plans, highway investments attracted much attention and their many shortcomings, because of their impact on national plan success, drew the planners' frequent attacks on agency structures and operations. The small housing programs, in contrast, drew little attention. Although they suffered in the scramble for scarce public resources, they were generally left alone to administer their very small piece of the public investment pie.

Despite these basic differences between the two agencies, they did share many structural and operational similarities that were representative of Central American bureaucracies as a whole. During the past two decades bureaucratic formalism, an important legacy of the hispanic tradition, actually expanded because of the need for greater central control over new agency operations. However, formal controls over expenditures and operations seldom resulted in the achievement of most professed policy objectives. And, despite formal centralization of authority in national governments, effective bureaucratic power often resided in the various government agencies. Consequently, budget decisions tended to conform to the relative power positions of agency directors rather than the weight of public demand. Civil service systems also met with little success because they threatened political patronage. Many legislators and most administrators opposed merit systems and, when forced to accept their enactment by planners and international agencies, they undermined their regulations.

The requirements of foreign assistance frequently threatened Central America's bureaucrats. The demands of international agencies for greater agency productivity placed them in a curious position. On the one hand, such demands strengthened agency budgetary bargaining power, for new foreign-financed projects required national counterpart funds. But, on the other hand, foreigners threatened the bureaucrats' paternalistic control with their demands for drastic changes in agency recruitment and operations. This dilemma, however, was not insoluble, for bureaucrats conveniently discovered "reorganization" as a means of coping with the external threat. Most reorganizations began with a flurry of activity led by foreign consultants, only to be followed a few years later by the discovery of the same structural problems by new consultants. This does not mean that Central American agencies completely failed to improve their performance, for many did improve. But such improvement was usually the result of gradual change that did not attack the paternalistic control system, rather than the product of formal reorganization. Reorganization was primarily a means of complying formally with demands for change while actually preserving basic paternalistic structures. It temporarily satisfied critics but assured the continual flow of foreign assistance to agency projects.

The cause of bureaucratic shortcomings was as much financial as structural. The expansion of operations to manage new programs assumed increased financial support of those operations. But, as foreign loans for agency development projects increased, national budgetary support for agency operations failed to keep pace. To a large extent, new projects were added to the Central American policy arsenals without the concomitant expansion of the means for managing them. The emergence of this paradoxical behavior should not be too surprising. In weighing their development policy commitments against their scarce financial resources, Central American presidents tried to establish their own optimal policy mix. The cost/benefit ratio of accepting foreign assistance appeared quite high, for it offered development policy outputs supported primarily, in the short run at least, by new external resources. The cost/benefit ratio of expanding bureaucratic operations, in contrast, was not too favorable, for it required the expansion of revenues and expenditures, a task which encountered firm political opposition. The optimal policy mix of the Central American presidents, therefore, was not the maximization of their development program opportunities through the full support of new agency operations but the salvaging of as many of their programs as possible under their resource and operational constraints.

Central American planners were forced to tolerate the salvaging strategy pursued by their presidents. The latter worked within, not against the constraints imposed by their policy-making processes. To them, development policy success was not measured by the total mileage of road construction or the number of houses built, though much of both was constructed despite numerous obstacles, but by their own political survival. They did not radically alter their political or administrative structures, but sought to absorb and mold new demands and resources into acceptable policy outputs through the use of existing institutions. The process was not smooth nor the product completely satisfying to the planners who demanded rapid infrastructure development. But the planners and their international allies, lacking the power or the strategies to remove the many constraining conditions, were forced to accept, albeit reluctantly, development policy bits and pieces in place of the massive development programs they had proposed a decade before.

6

The Survival of Development Projects

WHEN ALL IS SAID AND DONE, the proof of a development policy's success is measured by the goods it delivers and their use by the public. To be sure, commitments by presidents and their planners to particular development policies can serve numerous other objectives. They can be symbolically important in themselves and may enhance support for presidents regardless of the actual policy outputs. They may also be used to satisfy foreign demands for evidence of governmental intentions to expand national economies. Yet, despite the variety of ends such development policy commitments may serve, their principal objective is the creation of observable policy outputs that aid development.

Every examination of policy outputs begins with one principal handicap. In most policy arenas it is impossible to identify the final output of policy-making. Yehezkel Dror reminds us of this problem when he points out that:

identifying the real output of any discrete policy is hindered by such problems as: 1) it is hard to conceptualize, describe, or even qualitatively identify many elements of real output; 2) it is impossible to quantify many elements of real output; 3) there are additional variables that interfere and make it difficult, and often impossible, to isolate specific effects of any policy; 4) the real outputs are dispersed over time; and 5) there are frequently chain results and spill over effects in many spheres of social activity.[1]

1. Yehezkel Dror, *Policy-Making Re-examined* (San Francisco: Chandler Publishing Company, 1968), pp. 36–37.

To deal with these difficulties one is forced to establish a cutoff point in the analysis of policy outputs. I have established such a cutoff point in the analysis of highway and housing policy by focusing on specific development projects. Development projects are visible and identifiable in both time and space. As Albert Hirschman informs us:

> the development project is a special kind of investment. The term connotes purposefulness, some minimum size, a specific location, the introduction of something qualitatively new, and the expectation that a sequence of further development moves will be set in motion. If they are in the public sector, development projects may additionally be defined as those units or aggregates of public investments that, however small, will evoke direct involvement by high, usually the highest political authorities. Development projects then are the privileged particles of the development process.[2]

In examining highway and housing projects as components in the policy implementation process, we are concerned with the similarities and differences in project behavior. No effort is made to add up the costs and benefits of projects and to rank them according to such indices. Instead, they will be examined as experiences that can be compared against common performance criteria. Two groups of conditions or criteria are used to structure the examination of highway and housing project behavior. For highways I will compare project histories and project costs, concentrating on the problem of unanticipated excess costs. In the analysis of housing projects I will focus on project costs and clientele responses, i.e., the selection and participation of public housing recipients.

HIGHWAY PROJECTS:
RECOGNITION OF THE POSSIBLE

Three types of highway projects have been included in the analysis: 1) national highway programs, i.e., main artery roads;

2. Albert O. Hirschman, *Development Projects Observed* (Washington, D.C.: The Brookings Institution, 1967), p. 1.

2) farm-to-market roads; and 3) regional integration highways, i.e., those forming the new road system developed in 1963 to support Central American economic integration. Nineteen highway projects were examined; all were financed by loans from international or regional agencies and they accounted for approximately 90 percent of the new highway construction in the region during the Development Decade. (See Table 21.)

Diverse conditions surround these nineteen highway projects. They were financed by four different international agencies, their costs and their size differed widely, and they were implemented by five different governments. If we compare all projects by examining these conditions as independent variables and their behaviors as dependent variables, we might expect to find a wide variation among the latter because of the variation among the former. That is, certain combinations of these conditions might lead to one pattern of delays and cost increases in some projects while another combination might lead to different patterns in other projects.

Contrary to our expectations, however, this is not the case. Instead, despite widely differing conditions, the behavior of all nineteen highway projects is quite similar. That is, they experienced similar patterns of delay and unexpected cost increases. Or stated another way, the behavior of projects financed by any one international agency differed very little from projects financed by others; large and expensive projects implemented by one government differed little from small ones implemented by other governments.

In searching for explanations of these phenomena we can identify two types of conditions that were apparent in all five countries during the Development Decade and, therefore, aid in explaining common project behavior. One type will be termed "process" factors, for it includes factors common to the policy-making processes of the five countries; the other type is "project-specific" factors, for it includes factors inherent in the structure of highway projects. To discover the impact of each of these types of conditions on patterns of project behavior, I will first examine patterns of delays and then focus on unexpected cost increases.

TABLE 21
Major Highway Projects, 1960–1970

Project	Loans[a]	Granting Agency
National Highways		
Costa Rica		
National Road Program	11.0	IBRD/IDA
El Salvador		
National Road Program	3.0	IDA
Guatemala		
Rio Hondo Road	8.15	USDLF/Eximbank
Honduras		
Northern Road	9.5	IBRD
Northern Road	10.0	IDB
Farm-to-Market Roads		
Costa Rica		
Farm-to-Market Roads	4.0	IDB
Honduras		
Farm-to-Market Roads	5.2	USAID
Nicaragua		
Plan Lechero	12.0	IDB
Regional Roads		
Costa Rica		
San Ramon-Rio Colorado	4.7	CABEI
Rio Colorado-El Coco	5.8	CABEI
El Salvador		
La Union-Honduras border	2.4	CABEI
La Cuchilla-Km. 35	2.35	CABEI
Guatemala		
El Rancho-Santa Elena	4.2	CABEI
Santa Elena-Coban	4.0	CABEI
Honduras		
Tela-La Ceiba I	4.5	CABEI
Tela-La Ceiba II	4.274	CABEI
El Triunfo-Nicaragua border	0.733	CABEI
Nicaragua		
Octal-Las Manos	2.857	CABEI
Puente Real-Honduras border	3.986	CABEI

[a]Figures in millions of dollars.

Source: unpublished information supplied by the Central American Bank, USAID, and the Central American highway agencies.

Project Delays

Delays in highway project execution occur during two stages: before construction and during construction. For analytical purposes these periods can be defined as: 1) the period from the authorization of the project loan to the initiation of construction; and 2) from the beginning of construction to conclusion.

Delays during the pre-construction period are illustrated by the eleven regional road projects financed by the CABEI, for which detailed data are available.[3] Delays are clearly revealed by a comparison of actual pre-construction periods with the "usual time" norm employed by CABEI and other international agencies for Central American highway projects.[4] In Table 22 the actual time required to complete the preconstruction period on each project is listed. The pattern of delay is obvious; in all cases but one the eleven-month norm was exceeded.

A variety of process conditions account for most of these delays, although project-specific factors also affected some. The conditions clustered around three decision-making points in each of the projects. First, and most important, were delays resulting from ministerial decision-making. For example, in Guatemala delays were caused by disagreements among ministers and in El Salvador and Honduras by ministerial changes. The second decision-making point was the legislative process. In El Salvador and Costa Rica political opposition to presidential initiatives delayed loan agreement ratification by national legislatures. The

3. Similar detailed data on project schedules are not available for the other eight highway projects under examination.

4. Based on an estimated average of the time needed to complete all pre-construction activities, the "usual time" norm used by CABEI is eleven months. CABEI administrators argue that based on other Latin American experiences, all of the regional highway projects should be under construction within eleven months after a loan is granted. These activities include: 1) ratification of the loan agreement by the national legislature; 2) the selection of consultants; 3) the prequalification of contractors; 4) the awarding of contracts; 5) and the mobilization of the contractor and his equipment. See USAID, "Capital Assistance Paper: Central American Regional Highway Program," mimeographed (Washington, 1968).

TABLE 22
Highway Project Pre-Construction Periods

Project	Authorization	Start Const.	Time (mos.)
Costa Rica			
San Ramon-Rio Colorado	5/26/66	1/68	19
Rio Colorado-El Coco	3/09/67	1/69	20
El Salvador			
La Union-Honduras	5/26/66	11/68	29
La Cuchilla-Km. 35	5/26/66	11/68	29
Guatemala			
El Rancho-Santa Elena	5/26/66	12/66	5
Santa Elena-Coban	3/09/67	7/68	15
Honduras			
Tela-La Ceiba I	5/26/66	12/68	30
Tela-La Ceiba II	5/26/66	10/68	28
El Triunfo-Nicaragua	5/26/66	1/69	31
Nicaragua			
Octal-Las Manos	12/19/64	2/69	50
Puente Real-Honduras	12/19/64	3/66	15

Source: USAID, "Capital Assistance Paper: Central American Regional Highway Program," mimeographed (Washington, 1968), pp. 1–30.

third decision-making point was the procurement of consultants by the highway agencies. In El Salvador and Guatemala delays resulted from indecision over the selection of consultants. In general then, the principal delays centered around legislative and executive inaction resulting from internal conflicts and changes in political and administrative leadership.[5] The CABEI eleven-month norm, which naively assumed national consensus and administrative stability, was not met because its assumptions were incorrect. Each highway project opened new issues, required new resource allocation choices, and offered new threats as well as opportunities to highway agencies.

Project-specific delays are less significant, but not uncommon during the pre-construction period. Most centered around disputes over highway design. Very often last-minute adjustments were suggested by the consultants and were frequently disputed

5. Ibid.

by highway administrators. The most common dispute concerned the quality of road construction. Central Americans frequently argued for low quality standards in order to build longer roads with existing resources; most consultants, in contrast, demanded higher standards which required less maintenance work.

One of the most notorious examples of project-specific delay was Honduras' Northern Road project. Ten years of discussion and debate between Hondurans and consultants over the highway route preceded the initiation of construction in 1967. What began as a relatively simple process of route selection turned into a marathon of proposals and counter-proposals. It started with Honduran acceptance of a consultant's feasibility report in 1956. No further action was taken until 1961 when another American consultant was hired to make a general survey of long-range Honduran highway needs. Among its recommendations was a suggested change in the route of the Northern Road selected by the first consultant in 1956. These recommendations were supported by the findings of a third consultant who made a more detailed study of the Northern Road project in 1964.

In July 1965 the Hondurans signed IDB and IBRD loans to finance the project. Yet, before initiating construction highway officials decided to compare the findings of the 1957 and 1964 studies once again. A fourth consultant was hired to compare the two routes. This fourth consultant concluded that the original 1956 route was $4.5 million less expensive and shorter by 18 kilometers. After a flurry of negotiations, the IBRD and the IDB, in an unusual reversal of a loan contract decision, agreed to accept the 1956 route now supported by the Hondurans and their fourth consultant.[6]

The Honduran experience illustrates another problem faced by Central American presidents and their planners. Possessing little national expertise, they are often at the mercy of competing private consultants. Frequently, one president will commission a study by one consultant only to have his successor commission his own consultant for another study. What begins as a rather

6. "Report on the Comayagua-Potrerillos Highway Route: Northern Highway Project," submitted by Brown and Root, Inc., mimeographed (Tegucigalpa, 1967).

simple technical decision terminates as an expensive and time-consuming policy-making morass.

Most of the delays that occur during the second, or construction stage, of project execution were the products of project-specific factors. The most common in Central America were climatological conditions, particularly rainy seasons. But while the rainy season was often taken into account in project schedules, delays caused by contractor problems were not. Frequently contractors fell behind schedule because of equipment breakdowns or underestimation of required construction time. In the Costa Rican National Road Program some contractors went bankrupt, while in Guatemala the Rio Hondo Road contractor quit the project after a dispute with Guatemalan officials only to be persuaded to return again by USAID officials.

Project Costs

The second criterion for evaluating highway project behavior, project costs, also reveals deviations from expected performance patterns. To analyze project costs, the National Road and Farm-to-Market Road Programs were examined; the Regional Road Program, initiated in the late 1960s, was still in its initial construction phases and did not yet permit detailed cost analysis.

In every case examined, actual project costs far exceeded original cost estimates. In fact, all projects shared a common experience of unanticipated cost increases. First, estimates of project costs were made by national highway administrators, often with the assistance of foreign consultants. Next the project loan was granted by the international agency, and the project, after overcoming initial delays, progressed as planned during its first year. But during the second or third year of construction highway administrators suddenly discovered that construction costs per kilometer had risen much higher than anticipated. Reacting to their discovery, Central American presidents, already burdened by excessive demands on their budgets, refused to appropriate additional funds to cover the cost increase. Instead, they turned to the international agencies and asked for additional loans to cover the newly discovered cost increases. Only Guatemala's Rio Hondo Road, however, succeeded in gaining additional loan support. In all other cases the international agencies refused additional support and the projects were terminated when loan funds were exhausted, far short of construction goals. Thus, the Costa Ricans completed only 373 of 670 kilometers of their National Road Program and 317 of 610 of their Farm-to-Market Road Program.[7] Similarly the Nicaraguans were forced to reduce their Plan Lechero Program from 445 to 223 kilometers.[8] The Hondurans had to drop three of sixteen roads from their Farm-to-Market Road Program and the Salvadorians eliminated four of thirteen projects included in their National Road Program.[9]

Like project delays, unanticipated cost increases were the products of both project-specific and process conditions. The most common among the former was the underestimation of costs by highway agency technicians and their consultants. In part such problems were the natural product of the rapid expansion of highway construction in unfamiliar terrain by national and foreign technicians with little experience on large projects in the Central American region. At the same time, the Central American highway administrators readily admitted that deliberate cost underestimation was frequently used to encourage foreign agencies to grant loans for desperately needed, but very expensive projects. They argue that if they had announced the actual cost of the project, international agencies, in applying their own cost/benefit criteria, might have discovered that the costs exceeded the immediate benefits and refused to grant loans or demanded alterations in the projects. By underestimating costs they believed they could present, in the short run at least, a stronger case for project loan support.

The principal process-related condition was the fiscal crisis of the late 1960s and its impact on project financing. Central Ameri-

7. República de Costa Rica, Ministerio de Transportes, *Evaluación del plan vial: programa de carreteras nacionales y regionales* (San José, 1967), pp. 1–3; and *Evaluación del plan vial: plan de caminos vecinales* (San José, 1967), pp. 1–4.

8. República de Nicaragua, Ministerio de Fomento y Obras Públicas, *Evaluación integral del plan camabocho* (Managua, 1968), pp. 2–3.

9. USAID, *Honduras: Farm-to-Market Roads, Monthly Monitoring Report* (Tegucigalpa, 1968).

can presidents initially supplied counterpart funds for most projects, but as projects exceeded their original cost estimates they were unable, largely because of fiscal constraints, to cover the additional costs. Instead, as we have seen, they took the alternative path of reducing project size.

One indicator of the impact of fiscal constraints on project behavior is presidential budgetary support for annual highway investments. In all countries highway investments fell far short of the objectives proposed in the Five Year Plans. Between 1965 and 1967 highway investment averaged only 38 percent of planned levels in Costa Rica, 49 percent in El Salvador, 50 percent in Guatemala, and 42 percent in Honduras.[10]

Some important questions are raised by these patterns of highway investment performance. It seems that Central American presidents were willing to initiate new projects but failed to support their implementation. In essence, they seem to have made the easy choices, but floundered on the difficult ones. It appears, then, that Central American presidents cynically committed themselves to popular projects only to abandon them and their planners when difficulties arose.

Despite the obvious appeal of this "cynical presidents" interpretation of resource allocation and project management, an alternative view offers a more plausible explanation. One can argue that Central American presidents were pursuing the most viable strategy permitted by their resource constraints. The problems of project failure, excessive costs, and frequent delays are important components of this presidential strategy. If a president knows that he cannot supply sufficient funds for a highway project or that his agency cannot rapidly and effectively manage it, yet he sincerely wants it, what can he do? Obviously, he cannot admit probable project failures in his negotiations with international agencies, but neither can he undertake the project without foreign financing. Fully aware of his needs and constraints, he chooses a path that guarantees some foreign support and partial project completion. First, his engineers will underestimate the

10. Data supplied by the planning agencies of Costa Rica, El Salvador, Guatemala, and Honduras. After 1966 the Nicaraguans stopped publishing such information.

cost of the project (either out of ignorance or deliberately) to convince the international agency of its low cost and high benefits. Second, the president signs a loan and promises to comply with all loan requirements. After a couple of years cost overruns and national budgetary shortages take their toll. The president then takes two actions: he first seeks supplementary foreign loans, but if that fails, he merely eliminates the remaining parts of the original project that would have to be covered with the additional national funds that he cannot supply. Both courses of action were common in Central America: supplementary funds were given to Guatemala's Rio Hondo project, while in Costa Rica's National Road Program, El Salvador's National Road Program, and Nicaragua's Plan Lechero parts of the projects were dropped.

Despite the appearance of failure, the president, in pursuing this strategy, actually succeeds in completing a large part, if not all, of a project despite his resource constraints. To some this policy-making strategy appears irresponsible, but to others it reflects clever statesmanship, for the president not only succeeds in producing a beneficial policy output under adverse conditions, but he also manipulates the international agency into the fulfillment of its essential function, i.e., the subsidization of development in low income countries.

HOUSING PROJECTS: PICKING UP THE PIECES

The initiation of housing programs was preceded by the discovery of a "housing problem." Through housing censuses conducted during the early 1960s, "housing deficits" were identified in each country. (See Table 23.) Using standards of space, sanitation, and safety developed by the Pan American Union, housing officials discovered a regional deficit of nearly 1.5 million units, 384,481 of which were in urban areas. In response to political pressures, the advice of international agencies, and the economics of concentrated, large-scale production, the five governments ignored rural housing needs and focused their policy-making almost entirely on the urban housing problem. Their goal was a rapid reduction in the urban housing deficit by the end of the Development Decade. Their strategy consisted of the construction

TABLE 23
Estimated Housing Deficits

| | Deficient Houses | | Percent of region |
	Urban	Total	
Costa Rica (1963)	14,000	87,000	6
El Salvador (1961)	95,367	333,614	23
Guatemala (1964)	176,634	612,546	42
Honduras (1961)	36,600	249,300	17
Nicaragua (1963)	661,880	181,693	12
Total	384,481	1,464,153	100

Source: Banco Centroamericano de Integración Ecónomica, *Hacia un programa de vivienda urbana para centroamerica* (Tegucigalpa, 1967), p. 35.

of housing projects near major cities; each of these projects was to include a few hundred housing units that would be sold to low income families for between $1000 and $5000 through low interest, twenty-year mortgages.

The achievements of the five housing agencies fell short of their housing program goals for the decade. The average annual output of the housing agencies between 1960 and 1969 ranged from a high of approximately 1,500 units in El Salvador to a low of approximately 400 units in Honduras. With little help from the private sector, the housing agencies managed to stay only slightly ahead of urban population growth. Consequently, at the end of the decade the urban housing deficit remained approximately the same as it had been in 1960.

Despite their failures to reach program objectives, however, the housing agencies succeeded in constructing much badly needed housing for the region's urban poor. We are therefore concerned not only with their shortcomings, but also with their accomplishments. In particular we are interested in the general pattern of housing project behavior in the five countries. Two criteria, project costs and clientele responses, have been used in the evaluation of project behavior. The area under examination is the eight housing programs financed by the Inter-American Development Bank under the Alliance for Progress. These eight projects accounted for nearly all of the housing programs undertaken by the housing agencies during the decade. (See Table 20 in Chapter 5.)

Unlike highway projects, housing projects did not share similar patterns of behavior. Instead, their behavior has varied along both cost and clientele-response criteria. The variations have occurred, interestingly, from country to country rather than from project to project. In addition, policy-process conditions rather than project-specific factors appear to account for these variations in project behavior.

Project Costs

Cost problems affecting housing projects occurred only in Costa Rica and El Salvador, where firm housing policy commitments were made and the region's largest programs undertaken. In Costa Rica presidents failed to supply sufficient matching funds for IDB financed projects because of fiscal constraints and changing investment priorities; in El Salvador housing projects faced unanticipated cost increases because of excess administrative costs.

Governmental fiscal crisis was the principal process-related condition that affected Costa Rican housing projects. The fiscal problems that plagued the Orlich and Trejos administrations have already been discussed in Chapters 4 and 5. Orlich, it will be recalled, reduced the housing agency's budgetary subsidy in 1963 and used part of an USAID program loan to fulfill his subsidy obligation.[11] One of the principal victims of Orlich's robbing-Peter-to-pay-Paul budgetary techniques was the agency's IDB financed housing project. As Orlich failed to disburse all of the subsidy in 1964 and 1965, the agency's rate of construction began to decline. Then, in 1967, soon after Orlich's conservative successor José Trejos was inaugurated, the housing agency was en-

11. The USAID loan was intended for new housing projects, but President Orlich used it both for the new projects and his budgetary subsidy to the housing agency. This double use of the same funds contributed to poor performance in the implementation of the USAID projects. An audit in 1968 revealed that not all of the proposed units had been constructed and that the housing agency had rented rather than sold some units.

gulfed by a financial crisis. By 1967 the agency had utilized all of the $3.5 million loan granted it by the IDB in 1961, but, because of insufficient matching funds, it had constructed only 60 percent of the project's housing units.[12]

The Costa Ricans signed a second IDB loan for $3.6 million in 1965, but because of their failure to complete the first IDB loan, the IDB refused to disburse this second loan. The desperate housing agency board of directors, in order to prevent the collapse of its housing programs through the loss of IDB support, requested extraordinary budgetary support from the legislature and demanded that President Trejos pay all of his obligated 8 million *colones'* subsidy to the agency. Both the legislature and the president, however, ignored the board's request.[13]

The housing agency's only recourse was renegotiation of the two loans with the IDB. After extensive discussion the IDB agreed to declare the project "completed" after 3,875 of the programmed 5,725 units were constructed and to transfer the remaining units to the second loan-supported project. The IDB concessions, however, were not given without costs to the Costa Ricans. The housing agency agreed to grant the IDB authority to approve all future foreign loans and the purchase of all property for new projects. Thus, to compensate for their president's failure to support housing projects adequately, Costa Ricans had to relinquish much of their national control over public housing policy.

The Salvadorians, also victims of cost problems, did not suffer so much as the Costa Ricans. Their problems were of a different origin. They encountered unexpected cost increases of 25 percent in their self-help programs because of added demands for project supervision. They tried to adjust by reducing the number of self-help programs, but they were prevented from doing so by the IDB which had insisted upon them as part of the original loan contract. Then as fiscal conditions deteriorated, the agency's budgetary support was reduced to its lowest level of the decade, causing the housing agency to achieve only 30 percent of its in-

12. República de Costa Rica, INVU, *Prestamo 4/TF: informe del progreso del primer trimestre de 1968* (San José, 1968).

13. República de Costa Rica, INVU, *Dictamen del Consejo Técnico Consultivo* (San José, 1967).

vestment goals in 1966 and 12 percent in 1967.[14] Finally, the Salvadorians requested a third housing project loan from the IDB in 1968, but the IDB refused to grant the loan until the Salvadorians completed implementation of all existing self-help programs.[15]

The Guatemalans, Hondurans, and Nicaraguans, with much smaller projects, did not share the cost problems of the Costa Ricans and Salvadorians. In Guatemala and Honduras the programs were small and were initiated late in the decade; consequently, neither program made substantial claims on national budgets. The reasons for the Nicaraguans' avoidance of cost problems differ slightly from those of Guatemala and Honduras. The Nicaraguans, as we have seen, tied their development programs closely to the offerings of international agencies and gave higher priority to governmental financial stability than to the pursuit of welfare policies. The Nicaraguan housing agency was closely supervised by the nation's conservative Central Bank, which maintained very tight financial management of all housing projects. To their credit the Nicaraguans not only disbursed their first IDB housing loan on schedule, but they even saved enough money to construct 213 more housing units than planned under the loan agreement. Nicaraguan officials claim that they implemented housing projects more on a businesslike basis than did the other Central American governments because they were not confronted by political pressures for high production levels. When judged only on the cost criterion, they performed very well. Yet, as will be demonstrated below, the Nicaraguans paid a price for their efficient performance in terms of the relevance of their programs to the needs of their clientele.

A general pattern emerges from the analysis of housing project cost problems: the greater the claim of the housing program on the national budget the greater its vulnerability to national fiscal

14. República de El Salvador, IVU, *Solicitud de prestamo a BID* (San Salvador, 1968), pp. 10–11.

15. República de El Salvador, CONAPLAN, *Informe trimestral de proyectos de inversión pública al 31 de diciembre de 1967* (San Salvador, 1967) and *Informe trimestral de proyectos de inversión pública al 31 diciembre de 1967* (San Salvador, 1968).

problems. In the countries with large programs, i.e., Costa Rica and El Salvador, housing programs suffered the most. Although its symbolic value is important, public housing is one of the first items cut when austerity measures are imposed on public investment budgets. If the program is small and receives only enough appropriations to maintain a symbolic output of a few hundred units a year, it will likely survive austerity measures, for, if cut more, it would be entirely destroyed. Yet, it is also apparent that as these smaller programs grow, their vulnerability will likely increase. It is therefore doubtful that they will successfully expand unless new foreign or domestic resources can be consistently assured to them.

Clientele Responses

It is appropriate to examine clientele response when discussing housing project behavior, for public housing, much more than public highways, is constructed expressly to meet the social needs of a particular, underprivileged sector of the population. Consequently, project performance includes more than the construction of the project; it also involves the allocation of houses to needy beneficiaries.

The Central American housing agencies were created in the 1950s to meet the needs of the urban poor, but, as we have seen, because of financial constraints, they often fell short of their objectives. In addition, they have also fallen short because, in fulfilling the effective "demand" for housing, they did not respond to the "need" for housing. The determinant of this demand/need differential was family income. Under the IDB-financed programs the Central American housing agencies were to sell houses to families earning approximately $50 to $130 per month. In practice, however, they strongly favored those families with monthly incomes over $100. The consequences of this practice are obvious. Approximately 56 percent of the urban Central American families earn less than $90 monthly and 30 percent earn less than $50 monthly.[16] Thus, those most in need of housing—the poorest

16. Banco Centroamericana de Integración Económica, *Hacia Un programa de vivienda urbana para Centroamerica* (Tegucigalpa, 1965), p. 13.

urban families—did not qualify for it. Only those earning more than $50 monthly, and principally those earning at least $100 monthly, composed the effective demand for public housing.

Not only did the housing agencies not serve the most needy, but they began to abandon their original clients in search of less risky, higher income clients. As public housing recipients increasingly fell behind in their mortgage payments and threatened the financial stability of the housing agencies, frustrated housing officials sought to raise income qualifications even higher. Only Nicaragua, with the government most free of lower class political pressure, actually altered its policy in that direction. The Nicaraguan housing officials freely admitted that they were never satisfied with their low cost housing programs. As mortgage payment problems increased in the mid-1960s, so did their dissatisfaction. Finally in 1966 they raised the minimum income requirement from $50 to $107. Since approximately 70 percent of Nicaragua's urban families earned less than $107 monthly, the policy change removed public housing from the reach of a majority of those in need.[17] The official justification for the policy change, an increasingly persuasive one to troubled Central American public housing officials, was that "for a family with low income, job opportunities are fewer, security of employment is less, and its cultural level hinders responsible fulfillment of its obligations."[18]

Another clientele-related problem concerns the self-help approach to public housing construction. The self-help approach was designed, largely by IDB technicians, to meet the financial needs of low income families by offering them an opportunity to reduce the total cost of the house through the contribution of their own labor. In theory the client could provide up to 75 percent of the labor, but in Central American practice they have worked only six to ten hours on weekends in exchange for a 10 to 20 percent reduction in the house's total cost.

17. República de Nicaragua, Oficina de Planificación, *Plan nacional de desarrollo económico y social de Nicaragua 1965–1969*, parte II (Managua, 1965), p. 13.

18. República de Nicaragua, Banco de Vivienda Nicaraguense, *Informes del BNV al Presidente de la República: programa de vivienda popular para el periódo 1969–1972* (Managua, 1968), p. 2.

One would expect that self-help programs would be very popular in Central America, given the underemployment and poverty of the region. Recent experience indicates the opposite, however. Many of those who qualify for public housing are fully employed, sometimes at two or more jobs, and have little free time to work on their homes. In addition, housing officials discovered that because of the extensive supervision required by self-help projects, they were forced to compensate for their clients' savings through additional administrative expenditures.

Numerous problems were encountered in the implementation of self-help projects. In Nicaragua a 100-unit project was reduced to eleven units when most of the families withdrew, claiming that they could not fulfill their work obligations. In another project fifty-eight houses were started but only twenty-five completed. Displeased with the self-help project failures and their rising administrative costs, the housing agency decided to abandon them.[19] The Hondurans constructed approximately 50 percent of their first housing programs through self-help techniques, but because of administrative difficulties and decreasing client demand, only 10 percent of their second program used the self-help method. And, as we have seen, self-help programs accounted for the unexpected cost increases in the Salvadorian housing program. The Salvadorians tried to reduce their use of self-help procedure, but the IDB, the principal proponent of this approach, required Salvadorian use of the technique for the construction of half of the units in its second housing loan program.[20]

Central America's housing projects, despite their largely symbolic content, could not escape the problems that plagued the region's other development programs. The larger they were, the more they suffered from these financial and administrative obstacles. Fortunately, foreign assistance, which proved crucial for the execution of public housing policy during the Development Decade, rescued Central American presidents from the financial burdens of their housing policy commitments and guaranteed them visible symbols of governmental welfare policy. With the decline

19. Naciones Unidas, CEPAL, *Proyectos de esfuerzo propio y ayuda mutua en Centroamerica* (Mexico City, 1965).
20. Ibid.

in foreign assistance at the end of the decade, however, came stark realization that this seed capital had not produced the foundation for firm national housing programs. Instead, presidents found themselves trapped between the tradition of welfare paternalism and financial realities and were forced to shift housing programs to more reliable higher income urban families. By the end of the decade Central American presidents had altered their housing program objectives and had redirected their housing projects; their housing problem, however, remained unsolved.

THE PROBLEMS OF PROJECTS

In his study of eleven World-Bank-financed development projects Albert Hirschman concluded that: "it quickly became apparent to me that all projects are problem-ridden; the only valid distinction appears to be between those that are more or less successful in overcoming their troubles and those that are not."[21] The behavior of highway and housing projects in Central America supports Hirschman's findings; all projects encountered problems and some were overcome more easily than others.

Most striking about the Central American experience is the variety of causes of project problems. Technical problems associated with project design, engineering, and construction were frequent. But project implementation involved much more than these technical activities. Projects are particles of the public policy-making process and reflect most of its characteristics. Changes in political leadership, inter- and intra-ministerial disputes and legislative obstruction affected project implementation. As might be expected, fiscal policy also profoundly influenced project behavior. The task of project financing was particularly perplexing. On the one hand, presidents faced fiscal crises which prevented their full financial support of projects. Yet, even when they succeeded in meeting initial project costs, they often found themselves confronted by demands for even greater financial support to cover unanticipated project cost increases. The president's original policy commitment to a moderately priced project was

21. Hirschman, *Development Projects Observed*, pp. 2–3.

suddenly transformed into a burden of supporting an unexpectedly expensive one.

Hirschman, who analyzed projects from all over the world, could have been describing Central America when he wrote that " 'project implementation' may often mean in fact a long *voyage of discovery* in the most varied domains, from technology to politics."[22] Project implementation is a form of exploration surrounded by numerous uncertainties, and, despite their new programming and scheduling techniques, the Central American planners could not guide projects down certain and predictable paths. For, as Hirschman has observed, the planners "cannot even pretend to classify uniformally [sic], for purposes of decision-making, the various properties and probable lines of behavior of projects, as either advantages or drawbacks, benefits or costs, assets or liabilities."[23]

Given Hirschman's generalizations about project management and their added support from the Central American experience, one might conclude that Central American presidents must have been continually frustrated by their helplessness. But, in fact, that was not the case. While their planners persistently, and usually unsuccessfully, tried to reduce obstacles to policy implementation, presidents adjusted their expectations and agency directors their management of projects to accommodate the reality of recurring obstacles. In effect, they came to accept these obstacles as the predictable components of project implementation and administered their projects accordingly. Their acknowledgement of predictable obstacles is most clearly revealed by their management of highway projects, although it characterizes housing projects as well. Through their initial experience with highway projects in the late 1950s Central American policy-makers familiarized themselves with the conditions that affected their projects and they created policy-making strategies that recognized these conditions. Instead of remaining unanticipated threats, excessive costs and project delays became predictable components of project management. And as we have seen, presidents predicta-

22. Ibid., p. 35.
23. Ibid., p. 188.

bly requested additional funds from international agencies to compensate for their implementation problems and, when these were not supplied, they, just as predictably, reduced project size. This newly discovered predictablility of project behavior did not reduce project shortcomings. On the contrary, it only acknowledged them and guided presidents and administrators in the implementation of their strategy of partial success.

7

Conclusions

THE PURPOSE OF THIS STUDY has been the discovery of patterns of innovation and their consequences for policy-making processes. At its beginning three questions were raised: 1) why did the planners fail to achieve their public investment objectives? 2) why did an adversary rather than a cooperative relationship develop between planners and presidents? and 3) were there any differences in the performances of the five countries resulting from their different political systems?

Regarding the first question, our examination of the public investment decision sequence in Chapter 4 revealed that adverse economic conditions were the principal cause of persistent development program shortcomings. After recovering from a serious recession in the late 1950s the Central Americans initiated their Five Year Plans only to confront new adversity in the late 1960s as both external and internal economic conditions joined to reduce growth rates. Consequently, while public expenditures were rapidly rising, the rate of growth of public revenues and savings declined. Under similar conditions in the 1950s the region's presidents had manipulated internal and external credit to ease their financial plight, but this time they were not so fortunate. The semi-autonomous and conservative Central Banks, preaching their traditional doctrine of fiscal stability, balked at presidential pleas for rapid credit expansion and foreign assistance agencies, more hardened after four frustrating years of the Alliance for Progress, reduced their disbursement of loans to the region. Quite clearly, the development plans of the 1960s, like their economic policy predecessors, suffered from economic conditions beyond the control of the Central American presidents and their struggling planners.

THE PRESIDENTIAL CALCULUS

An answer to the second question is more elusive. Chapter 3 discussed the conflicts between presidents and planners that led to the increasing isolation of the latter. The form and impact of their antagonisms varied according to political norms within each country. In dictatorial Nicaragua the confrontation was the most intense and the rejection of the planners the most severe as an energetic planning director challenged a powerful president, who reacted by excluding the planner from inner policy-making councils. In conflict-ridden Guatemala, in contrast, a formal confrontation never really developed as the planners remained isolated from the beginning. In El Salvador, Costa Rica, and Honduras the battles were less intense and their consequences less severe. In none of the three was the planning agency completely suppressed nor totally isolated, but neither did it exercise influence over policy or bureaucracy. Frustrated planners came and departed with increasing frequency as they saw their policy and administrative innovations persistently ignored.

Despite these national variations, a general pattern of antagonism and isolation prevails in Central America and therefore the question remains: why this pattern and not one of gradual mutual accommodation like that described by Lindblom and Gross?

Central American politicians and administrators have been quick to supply one answer: the cause of their isolation lies with the planners themselves. These young *técnicos*, they argue, misunderstood and therefore resented politics and politicians from the beginning. They self-righteously proclaimed themselves the guardians of new development policies and demanded their unquestioning application by political leaders. When their naive programs were not applied, the *técnicos* withdrew from policy-making councils in disgust and blamed politics and the political leaders whom they mistakenly saw as selfish, old-fashioned manipulators of the public good.

This view, while comforting to those politicians who felt threatened by the planners, fails to consider much evidence to the contrary. That the *técnicos* aspired to a more rational or synoptic policy-making process cannot be denied, but they were hardly unaware of political realities and their impact on economic policy-making. Some *técnicos* had had first-hand experience with such realities through their work in regional agencies during the formative years of the Central American Common Market in the late 1950s. Moreover, most had also labored in national ministries before entering the planning offices. Their disillusionment came not only from their inability to apply the rational policy-making model, but also from daily rejection of their policy recommendations. Some, as we saw in the cases of Rivera in Honduras and Sacasa in Nicaragua, were often even refused an opportunity to debate policy proposals with cabinet ministers; instead they were assigned only the meager functions of preparing foreign loan applications and annual public investment reviews.

Rather than place all responsibility for the antagonism on the *técnicos*, we might focus on their principal adversaries—the Central American presidents whom they sought to influence. The presidents' resistance to planning and their frequent rejection of the *técnicos'* advice should not be surprising. If it is, that is so because we have been seduced by the belief that, because presidents of developing countries need economic programs to restructure and expand their economies, they will enthusiastically apply planning techniques to their policy-making processes. But that which is so compelling to outside observers, especially those from aid-granting industrial nations, is not equally compelling to the presidents of developing countries. To understand this difference we must examine more closely the political alternatives that confronted the Central American presidents.

The planners offered the Central American presidents new threats as well as opportunities. Each can be distinguished in an examination of what might be termed a presidential cost/benefit calculus of development policy-making. The prevailing assumption of such an analysis is that the president's principal objective is the preservation or expansion of his personal political power. First, let us examine the three major benefits offered by the planners since they are the most obvious.

1) RATIONAL ALLOCATION OF PUBLIC RESOURCES: Central American presidents professed to want economic development and an improvement in the living standard of their populations. The planners offered a means of attaining these objectives through their coordinated application of fiscal, monetary, exchange, and other policy instruments. Naturally, no planner would guarantee economic growth, but he would claim to make more efficient use of scarce resources to attain particular growth objectives.

2) CONSTRUCTION OF DEVELOPMENT PROJECTS: As a corollary to the above, the planners offered to supervise and coordinate the construction of badly needed public works to expand the region's social and economic infrastructure. Development projects were not only new contributions to national development, but also observable policy outputs that presidents could manipulate to secure popular support. New housing projects, for example could be deftly exploited to gain the approval of the urban poor while new roads could be presented to agricultural, industrial, and commercial interests as examples of presidential support for the private economic sector.

3) ATTRACTION AND MANAGEMENT OF FOREIGN ASSISTANCE: Since the initiation of the Alliance for Progress in 1961, national planning has been a prerequisite for most foreign assistance to Central America. While international agencies have been tolerant of many planning agency shortcomings, they have at least insisted on some planning in the hope that it would assure more effective management of foreign assistance. Planners therefore offered presidents greater opportunities for negotiating and securing the financial assistance they needed to support their burgeoning investment budgets and to relieve them temporarily from embarrassing fiscal crises.

Now let us turn to the political costs of planning which are less obvious than the three benefits but were more instrumental in the planners' failure to influence policy decisions.

1) THREAT TO DOMINANT INTEREST GROUPS: The planners' proposals frequently threatened the interests of the presidents' most important supporters. As we have seen repeatedly, the Central American presidents, although calling themselves reformers, did not seek significantly to redistribute resources. In fact they very carefully acknowledged the policy claims of their societies' most powerful groups, particularly those associated with export agriculture. The planners too initially avoided direct attacks on national economic structures or economic elites. Eventually, however, they found it necessary to recommend redistributive tax reforms to generate revenue for public investment programs. Although at first acquiescing to the planners' requests, in part because of the demands of international agencies, the presidents were later forced to rescind their tax reforms in order to maintain the support of major economic power contenders. The planners' reform demands also threatened bureaucratic power contenders within the government, forcing other executive officials to demand and gain the planners' exclusion from policy-making councils.

2) FEAR OF EXCESSIVE DEPENDENCE ON THE *técnicos*: Inherent in any expansion of the planners' influence on policy-making is the danger of increased presidential dependence on them. As commitments are made to long-range development programs, as the manipulation of policy instruments becomes more sophisticated, and as dependence on foreign assistance increases, presidents are forced to rely more heavily on their planners' judgments. The planners, however, were not part of the Central American presidents' personal following and usually possessed little loyalty to them. From the traditional viewpoint of the region's very personalistic presidencies, the planners did not merit the trust, and certainly not the dependence, of presidents. Consequently, in dealing with them, presidents frequently acted as if they had to guard carefully against the growth of such a dependency relationship. The result, of course, was presidential insulation from the planning agencies.

3) THREAT TO PATRONAGE POWERS: In their frustration with lax and inefficient program implementation the planners, as did the international agencies, focused their wrath on the national bureaucracies. Their annual plan reviews pointed to structural

deficiencies and incompetent personnel as the major causes of program delays and failures. To remedy the problem they demanded the replacement of presidential patronage powers with some form of merit system. Presidents formally acknowledged their complaints but took little remedial action because they could not eliminate patronage without damaging an important source of political support.

As presented above, the presidential cost/benefit calculus appears quite static. In reality, of course, it is not, for presidents continually weigh diverse demands, including those of the planners. The relative weight of political costs and benefits obviously varies from time to time depending on presidential perceptions and political conditions. What is so striking about the Central American experience, however, is the persistent pattern of costs outweighing benefits in the presidential calculus. In closely guarding their patronage powers and persistently yielding to the objections of traditional power contenders they have gradually isolated their planning agencies. The planners, quite simply, lacked clout in the policy-making process. Their most important political resource is their assistance in the presidential task of governing, but presidents did not need them to govern; on the contrary, they often had to deny them in order to stay in power.

THE POLITICAL ECONOMY OF PROGRAM FAILURE

One lingering question remains unanswered—what was the impact of political system differences on development program performance? For example, were authoritarian systems more effective in implementing development programs than democratic ones? Did the amount and form of political participation affect presidential policy choices? The analysis of the Central American experience, while limited in scope, adds some insight into these perennial questions. Throughout the region the goals of national development programs were quite similiar, calling for a rapid expansion of public investment primarily in economic infrastructure. At the same time, there were political system differences among the five countries which are most clearly revealed by the dimensions of political competition and stability. The Costa Rican system was characterized by very competitive political parties, a disbanded military, and constitutional stability. Equally stable but much less competitive were Nicaragua and El Salvador. Nicaragua was controlled by a strong personalistic presidency that manipulated the rules of political competition and used a small military force to perpetuate rule by the Somoza clan. El Salvador's more broadly based ruling party was directed by a military-civilian coalition which sought to preserve the economic power of the coffee planter oligarchy while satisfying at least a minimum of popular welfare demands. Honduras and Guatemala were the least stable of the five countries. The former was characterized by its very combative but decentralized two-party system and a military that moved from periodic intervention to the imposition of nominal stability through direct rule. Guatemala has suffered from intensely conflicting political forces, changing party configurations, and a military that has also rapidly expanded its participation in policy-making.

Certainly these diverse political characteristics must have yielded some differences in the performances of the five countries. Yet as we have seen, a single pattern of quantitative shortcomings, caused primarily by common economic problems, prevails in all five countries. But this does not mean that political system differences had no impact on development program performance, for if we move from aggregate measures of performance to more specific policy choices, we can observe some important performance variations.

Political system differences can be analyzed in terms of the constraints they imposed on presidential policy choices. In short, political conditions either permit certain latitudes or freedom for policy choice or they impose specific disciplines or constraints on them. In Central America their impact is most readily seen in the contrasting ways in which presidents managed their fiscal and development policy decisions when faced by a common set of unanticipated economic problems in the late 1960s.

The president's principal task during this period was political survival amid program failure. During each fiscal crisis he had to take at least three actions: 1) decide how much of his development program to cut and whom to hurt in reducing his budget;

2) publicly explain and justify his program cuts; and 3) respond to the policy demands and assistance offered by international agencies. By reviewing these presidential decisions we can identify and compare the latitudes and disciplines imposed by each political system.

Most illustrative, as it has been throughout the study, is the contrast between Costa Rica and Nicaragua. Since their 1948 revolution Costa Rican presidents have faced popular demands for the rapid expansion of social and economic services that have been repeatedly ratified by electoral and legislative processes. When faced by fiscal crisis the president has found his remedial policy options limited by popular expectations, past policy commitments, and active opposition to welfare policy reductions. Rather than reducing expenditures and risking opposition wrath, he tolerated fiscal crises and accepted financial reprisals for failing to implement foreign advice. In so doing he disarmed many of his critics, for by waiting for adverse foreign reaction to his own inaction the Costa Rican president succeeded in placing the blame for eventual program reductions on foreign agencies rather than on his own fiscal management.

No such devious strategy was required in Nicaragua. The Somozas had long suppressed popular claims for the extension of social services and were not threatened by a political opposition. Consequently, they reacted to fiscal problems by using their wide latitude for policy selection and sacrificed both economic and social programs in order to maintain financial stability and preserve their private business empire. In so doing they quite intentionally cultivated the praise and financial support of several foreign assistance agencies.

Honduran presidents enjoyed almost as much latitude as the Nicaraguans. To be sure, the military president who ruled through the Nationalist party during most of the decade faced occasional protest from the Liberal party opposition, but most complaints were either quickly suppressed or were lost amid the widely dispersed Honduran population. The Honduran president's policy-making latitude and relative fiscal stability during most of the decade offered him greater opportunity for new development policy departures than any of the other Central American presi-

Unfortunately, our analysis of the strengths and weaknesses of the five systems does not lead to the identification of a model policy-making system in which distributional and regulatory policy instruments could be managed equally well. Our problem is due to the complexity and diversity of policy-making itself. The Central American experience teaches the futility of statements about a particular level or form of participation being a sufficient condition for general program success. National development policy is the product of the selection of many objectives, some even in conflict with each other, and the application of several instruments, each of which thrives under different mixes of popular participation and central control. The policymaker does not construct a flexible policy-making process that is conducive to matching each policy instrument with its appropriate mix. Instead, he inherits political structures that result from decades of national development, political conflict, and bargains struck between major power contenders. Thus, the unrevolutionary Central American leaders did not have a blank slate on which to design new policy-making structures but accepted one already encumbered by well-established rules. Unable or unwilling to challenge these rules, they tolerated their adverse effects on development policies. In sum, we, along with the region's frustrated *técnicos*, have discovered not a new model but simply a familiar reality: during the Development Decade Central American political leaders did not fashion new policy-making structures, but only applied some new policy instruments in coping with the shortcomings of old ones.

REFERENCE
MATTER

A NOTE ON SOURCES

AS STATED IN THE ACKNOWLEDGMENTS, the cooperation of public officials greatly facilitates the analysis of public policy-making. This is particularly true in areas like Central America where governmental form and policy-making reality often differ widely. This study has benefitted immensely from the contributions of numerous national, regional, and international officials who have observed and affected Central American development during the past three decades. They have assisted the study in two ways: in informal interviews they described and explained their policy-making experiences; they supplied public documents, many of which could only be found in their personal files. Since the study draws so extensively on these two sources, their use requires some explanation in the following pages.

A. INTERVIEW DATA

My interviewing concentrated on a set of public officials who were directly involved with the policies and agencies I was studying. In each of the five countries these interviewees included: the director (and ex-directors) of the planning agency, his subordinates in charge of public investment, directors of housing and highway agencies and their principal subordinates, the director of the local Inter-American Bank office, the US Bureau of Public Roads representatives, and local USAID capital development officers. At the regional level I interviewed the highway and housing specialists of the Central American Bank and all members of the Common Market Secretariat's regional planning division. In addition, I also interviewed numerous local experts, e.g., private consultants, contractors, and local technicians not working for public agencies. In all approximately 100 people were interviewed in some depth.

The interview format proved crucial to the quality and quantity of information generated. My initial use of a semi-structured, formal interview technique proved unsatisfactory, for I quickly discovered through cross-checking that this approach elicited some polite and superficial commentary but little direct discussion of the problems and conflicts confronting officials. I then changed my technique to a much more informal one which proved immensely successful. Essentially, I requested and was granted permission in nearly all of the agencies under study to examine documents and files on agency premises. During the three or four days I spent in each agency I opportunely quizzed the relevant officials on questions raised by the documents and other matters that concerned me. I took notes during the day and typed them each night. In this way, I believe, I gathered and recorded crucial insights into the perceptions and behavior of public officials that are seldom elicited by the formal interview. I highly recommend the technique to researchers who possess the requisite language skills and enjoy a hospitable research environment.

While I have drawn extensively on the documents to support my arguments in the text, there are some descriptions and interpretations that depend largely on interview data. The exact citation of specific interviews proved impossible since anonymity was required because of the possible adverse political consequences of even remote associations of officials with their comments. Consequently, where interview data are crucial to my argument I have merely informed the reader of that fact in a note. I would have preferred more precise citation, but, like the Central American presidents, I too am constrained by some of the unfortunate realities of Central American politics.

B. PUBLIC DOCUMENTS

Public documents supplied general description, quantitative data, and critical analysis which answered many of the questions raised in the study. For the description and analysis of development plan performance, particularly along quantitative dimensions, I have drawn largely on the informative annual plan reviews written since 1965 by the national planning agencies. The researcher cannot help but admire and appreciate the Central American planners' willingness to share these frank and self-critical documents with the intruding foreign scholar. I only hope that this study aids in answering a few of the questions that concern these dedicated men.

My analysis of the general planning and development policy-making processes has benefitted from the excellent annual "country reviews" made since the early 1960s by the Inter-American Committee of the Alliance for Progress. These reports appear in two forms: a general study of development progress by the Organization of American States Secretariat, entitled "Domestic Efforts"; and the text of a discussion among country officials, representatives of international agencies, and the OAS Secretariat team, entitled "Final Report of the CIAP Subcommittee."

In my examination of development projects I have used the project evaluations and loan reports undertaken by private consultants and international agencies. These materials both satisfy and frustrate the researcher. They contain some of the most detailed and revealing analyses of individual projects now available, but they are frequently the most difficult to find. Most international agencies, preoccupied with immediate problems, have neglected the systematic collection and filing of their project reports. In the absence of such efforts the task of collecting and comparing project reports and explaining project behaviors goes by default to the independent researcher.

Clearly, this study demonstrates the utility of a host of new documentary sources available to the student of development policy. Their variety can be seen in the following bibliography of documents consulted for this book.

General

Banco Centroamericano de Integración Económica [BCIE].
Análisis sobre servicios de ingenería para proyectos de factibilidad y de inversión en centroamerica financiados por el BCIE. Tegucigalpa, Honduras, 1968.
Hacia un programa de vivienda urbana para Centroamerica. Tegucigalpa, 1965.
Informes de actividades counsultores. Tegucigalpa, Honduras, 1969.
Plan vial centroamericano y solicitudes de prestamo. Tegucigalpa, Honduras, 1962.
Principales modalidades del credito inmobiliario en Centroamerica. Tegucigalpa, Honduras, 1967.
Escuela Superior de Administración Pública para América Central [ESAPAC].
Diagnostico y macro análisis administrativos del sector público del Istmo Centroamericano. San José, Costa Rica, 1965.
Las dilemas de la descentralización funcional: un análisis de la autonomia institucional pública, por Wilberg Jimenez Castro. San José, Costa Rica, 1965.
Estudio critico de la ESAPAC: sus objectivos y programas, por Jose Calvan Escobedo. San José, Costa Rica, 1962.
Importancia de la modernización de la administración pública para el programa de integración del Istmo Centroamericano, por Wilberg Jimenez Castro. San José, Costa Rica, 1967.
Informe de la conferencia para la determinación de prioridades

en la accion administrativa estatal para el desarrollo. San José, Costa Rica, 1964.

Informe del seminario regional de administración de programas de construcción y mantenimiento de carreteras. San José, Costa Rica, 1965.

Informe del seminario sobre administración para el desarrollo. San José, Costa Rica, 1963.

Informe del seminario sobre organización y administración de carreteras. Tomo 1. San José, Costa Rica, 1961.

Instituto Centroamericano de Administración Pública [ICAP].

Informe de la primera reunion de Directores Generales de Caminos del Istmo Centroamericano. San José, Costa Rica, 1967.

El mejoramiento administrativo: para que? San José, Costa Rica, 1969.

Necesidades de personal en el sector público de Centro América: 1974. San José, Costa Rica, 1969.

Recursos humanos: el sector público y su situación actual en Centro América. San José, Costa Rica, 1968.

Inter-American Development Bank [IDB].

Eighth Annual Report. Washington, 1967.

Social Progress Trust Fund Annual Reports. Washington, 1962, 1963, 1964, 1965, 1966, 1967, 1968, 1969.

Naciones Unidas. Comision Económica para América Latina [CEPAL].

Evaluación de la integración económica en Centroamérica. Mexico City, 1966.

Proyectos de esfuerzo propio y ayuda mutua en Centroamérica. Mexico City, 1965.

El transporte en América Latina. Tomo 1. Mexico City, 1965.

El transporte en el Istmo Centroamericano. Mexico City, 1953.

Comite de Cooperacion Económica del Istmo Centroamericano.

Financiamiento de la vivienda en el Istmo Centroamericano, por Carlos Leonidas Arevedo. Mexico City, 1965.

"La integración económica de Centroamérica." Mimeographed. 20 junio 1950; 16 junio 1951; 16 octubre 1953. Mexico City.

Situación del transporte en Centroamérica. Mexico City, 1958.

Subcomite de Vivienda, Edificación y Planeamiento del Istmo Centroamericano.

Informe de la primera reunion. Mexico City, 1958.
Informe de la tercera reunion. Mexico City, 1965.
Nicaragua, Instituto Nacional de Vivienda; Honduras, Instituto Nacional de Vivienda; El Salvador, Instituto de Vivienda Urbana; y Guatemala, Instituto Nacional de Vivienda.
"Comentarios al documento GN–140–1 del Banco Interamericano de Desarrollo." Letter to IDB, 1968.
Organización de Estados Americanos [OEA] Secretaria.
El avance de la integración centroamericana y las necesidades de finciamiento externo. Washington: Union Panamericana, 1968.
Progreso de la administracion para el desarrollo en America Latina. Washington: Union Panamericana, 1967.
    Union Panamericana. Division de Vivienda y Planamiento. Departamento de Asuntos Económicos y Sociales.
    La vivienda de interés social en América Latina. Washington: Union Panamericana, 1957.
Organization of American States [OAS].
    Inter-American Economic and Social Council. Ad-hoc Committee for the Study of the Low-Cost Housing Problems.
        Problems of Housing of Social Interest. Washington: Pan American Union, 1954.
    Pan American Union.
        Capital Formation for Housing in Latin America. Washington: Pan American Union, 1963.
        Farm to Market Roads in Latin America. Washington: Pan American Union, 1964.
        Department of Economic Affairs.
            General Problems of Transportation in Latin America. Washington: Pan American Union, 1963.
    Secretariat.
        Report on the Central American National Development Plans and the Process of Economic Integration. Washington: Pan American Union, 1966.
Secretaria Permanente del Tratado General de Integración Económica Centroamericana [SIECA].
"Algunas medidas practicas y estrategicas en la ejecución presupuesta." Mimeographed. IV Reunion de Directores de Presupuesto de Centroamerica, Tegucigalpa, Honduras. Guatemala, 1967.

Cinco años de labores en la integración económica centroamericana. Guatemala, 1966.

Estudio sobre mantenimiento regional de carreteras centroamericanas. Guatemala, 1966.

Evaluación de los sistemas presupuestarios de centroamérica. IV Reunion de Directores de Presupuesto de Centroamerica, Tegucigalpa, Honduras. Guatemala, 1967.

Informe del reunion de Ministros de Economía y de Obras Públicas. Guatemala, 1963.

Informe preliminar: programa regional de carreteras centroamericanas. Tomo 1. Guatemala, 1963.

Informe sobre el progreso del programa centroamericano de carreteras. Guatemala, 1965.

Memorandum: Perspectivas del ahorro y la inversion del sector público para los años de 1967, 1968, 1969. Guatemala, 1966.

Peculiaridades técnicos-administrativos de los programas viales centroamericanos, por Ing. Modesto Armijo Mejia. Reunion de Ministros de Economía y de Obras Públicas, Guatemala. Guatemala, 1963.

Quinto compendio estadistico centroamericana. Guatemala, 1967.

Comite Asesor de Planificación Para Centroamerica, Septima Reunion.

Actividades de la division de desarrollo, 1966–67. Guatemala, 1967.

Mision Conjunta de Programación para Centroamerica.

Centroamerica: inversiones públicas en 1965. Guatemala, 1964.

Resumen de los planes centroamericanos de desarollo económico y social para el periodo 1965–69. Guatemala, 1966.

Resumen de los programas centroamericanos de inversiones públicas. Guatemala, 1965.

United Nations. Economic Commission for Latin America [ECLA]. "Economic Policy and Planning in Latin America." Mimeographed. E/CN. 12/711. Santiago, Chile, 1965.

Economic Survey of Latin America—1964, 1965, 1966, 1967, 1968. New York, 1965, 1966, 1967, 1968, 1969.

"Report of the Central American Economic Cooperation Committee." Mimeographed. E/CN. 12/552. 3 September 1959–13 December 1960. Mexico City, 1961.

United States.
> Department of State. Agency for International Development.
> "Capital Assistance Paper: Central American Regional
> Highway Program." Mimeographed. Washington, 1968.
> Congress. Senate.
> > Committee on Foreign Relations. Subcommittee on
> > American Republics Affairs.
> > > *Survey of the Alliance for Progress.* 91st Cong., 1st
> > > sess., S. Doc. 91–17. Washington, 1969.
> > Committee on Government Operations. Subcommit-
> > tee on Foreign Aid Expenditures.
> > > *United States Foreign Aid in Action: A Case Study.*
> > > 89th. Cong., 2nd sess., Committee Print. Wash-
> > > ington, 1966.
> Department of Transportation. Bureau of Public Roads.
> > *A Brief Report on the Inter-American Highway.* Wash-
> > ington, 1963.

World Bank.
> International Bank for Reconstruction and Development
> [IBRD].
> > *The World Bank in Latin America.* Washington, 1960.
> and International Development Association [IDA].
> > *Economic Development and Prospects of Central America.*
> > Vol. 1, *Main Report.* Washington, 1967.

Costa Rica

LAWS

"Ley de Planificación, Num. 3087." January 31, 1963.
"Ley Num. 3155." August 5, 1963.
"Ley Organica del Instituto Nacional de Vivienda Urbana." 1954.

OFFICIAL GOVERNMENT PUBLICATIONS

Instituto Nacional de Vivienda Urbana [INVU].
> *Debemos financiar nuestras programas de vivienda unicamente
> con prestamos internacionales?* San José, Costa Rica, 1957.
> *Dictamen del Consejo Técnico Consultivo.* San José, Costa Rica,
> 1967.

Memorias, 1956, 1961, 1962, 1964, 1965, and 1966. San José, Costa Rica.

"Prestamo 4 TF: Informe de progreso del primer trimestre de 1968." Mimeographed. San José, Costa Rica, 1968.

Ministerio de Economía y Hacienda. Oficina del Presupuesto.
Informes, 1960, 1961, and 1962. San José, Costa Rica.

Oficina de Organización y Métodos.
Manual de organización de la administración pública de Costa Rica. San José, Costa Rica, 1962.
Proyecto para reorganizar el Ministerio de Obras Públicas. San José, Costa Rica, 1962.

Ministerio de Obras Públicas.
Estudios sobre la primera etapa del plan vial. San José, Costa Rica, 1961.
Memoria, 1954. San José, Costa Rica, 1965.

Ministerio de Transportes.
Contrato para la construcción y mejoramiento de caminos vecinales. San José, Costa Rica, 1964.
Evaluación del plan vial: programa de caminos vecinales. San José, Costa Rica, 1967.
Evaluación del plan vial: programa de carreteras nacionales y regionales. San José, Costa Rica, 1967.
Memoria 1962–1966. San José, Costa Rica, 1967.
Reseña historica de los transportes en Costa Rica. San José, Costa Rica, 1967.

Presidencia de la República. Oficina de Planificación, [OFIPLAN].
Comentario sobre la ejecución del Plan Nacional de Desarrollo, 1965–1968. San José, Costa Rica, 1964.
Observaciones a la ejecución del Plan Nacional de Desarrollo, 1965–1968. San José, Costa Rica, 1968.
Plan de Desarrollo Económico y Social de Costa Rica 1965–1969. San José, Costa Rica, 1964.
Previsiones del desarrollo económico y social de Costa Rica y planes del sector público para 1969–1972. Version Preliminar. San José, Costa Rica, 1969.
Situación y perspectivas de la economía costarricense: programas a ejecutar en 1968 y sus bases presupuestarias. San José, Costa Rica, 1968.

Departamento de Coordinación y Control.
Control y evaluación del programa de inversiones públicas 1967. San José, Costa Rica, 1968.
Control del programa de inversiones públicas 1966. San José, Costa Rica, 1967.
Informe sobre el control del programa de inversiones públicas 1965. San José, Costa Rica, 1966.
Plan operativo anual de inversiones públicas 1969. San José, Costa Rica, 1968.
Departamento de Planes Anuales.
Informes, 1963, 1964, 1965, 1966. San José, Costa Rica.
Presupuesto regional centroamericano. San José, Costa Rica, 1966.
Departamento de Productividad y Eficiencia Administrativa.
Informe de labores. San José, Costa Rica, 1967.
"Ministerio de Transportes: Reorganización administrativo." Mimeographed. San José, Costa Rica, 1968.
And United States Bureau of Public Roads.
"Inter-American Highway Monthly Narrative Report." Mimeographed. San José, Costa Rica, 1959.
"Inter-American Highway Monthly Report of Activities." Mimeographed. San José, Costa Rica, 1968.

OTHER PUBLICATIONS

Instituto Centroamericano de Administración Pública.
Estudio sobre las instituciones autonomias de Costa Rica. San José, Costa Rica, 1967.

Organizacion de Estados Americanos.
Costa Rica y las metas de la Alianza para El Progreso. Washington: Pan American Union, 1969.
Union Panamericana. Comité ad hoc Alianza para el Progreso.
Evaluación del Plan de Desarrollo Económico y Social de Costa Rica 1965–1968. Washington: Union Panamericana, 1965.

Organization of American States.
"Final Reports of the CIAP Sub-Committee on Costa Rica." Mimeographed. February, 1966; January, 1967; December, 1967; October, 1968. Washington: Pan American Union.

Secretariat.
"Domestic Efforts and the Needs for External Financing
for the Development of Costa Rica." Mimeographed.
September, 1966; October, 1967; September, 1968.
Washington: Pan American Union.

United States. Department of Transportation. Bureau of Public
Roads.
"Highway Maintenance in Costa Rica." Mimeographed. Report by
Technical Assistance Staff. San José, Costa Rica, 1968.

World Bank. International Bank for Reconstruction and Development.
"Current Economic Position and Prospects of Costa Rica." Mimeographed. Report. No. WH 54–A. 1967.

El Salvador

LAWS

"Decreto Legislativo de 29 de Mayo." 1926.
"Decreto Num. 111." December 29, 1950.
"Decreto Num. 346." October 23, 1961.
"Decreto Num. 59." April 1962.
"Ley de Salarios, 1949."
"Ley de Salarios, 1966–1967."

OFFICIAL GOVERNMENT PUBLICATIONS

Consejo Nacional de Planificación y Coordinación Económica
[CONAPLAN].
Informe trimestral de proyectos de inversión pública al 31 de diciembre de 1965. San Salvador, 1966.
Informe trimestral de proyectos de inversión pública al 31 de diciembre de 1966. San Salvador, 1967.
Informe trimestral de proyectos de inversión pública al 31 de diciembre de 1967. San Salvador, 1968.
Plan de la Nación 1965–1969. San Salvador, 1964.

Instituto de Vivienda Urbana [IVU].
Forma de financiamiento en los programas de viviendas de 1951 a 1967. San Salvador, 1968.
Memorias 1958, 1959–1960, 1961–1967. San Salvador.
Solicitud de prestamo a BID. San Salvador, 1968.
Viviendas construidos por el Instituto. San Salvador, 1968.

Ministerio de Obras Públicas.
  La Carretera del Litoral: Informe final de construcción. San Salvador, 1962.
  Memorias de Obras Públicas 1958–1959, 1960–1961, 1962–1963, 1964–1965, 1965–1966, 1966–1967, 1967–1968, San Salvador.
  Dirección General de Caminos.
    Concentraciones totales de costos por obras y por programas. San Salvador, 1968.
    "Engineering and Economic Feasibility Report: El Salvador National Highway Program." Mimeographed. By Tippetts-Abbett-McCarthy-Stratton Inter-American Corporation. San Salvador, 1961.
    Factibilidad de ingeniería y economía del programa regional de carreteras centroamericanas. San Salvador, 1965.
    "National Highway Program: Ministry of Public Works Progress Report No. 41." Mimeographed. San Salvador, 1966.

OTHER PUBLICATIONS

Organización de Estados Americanos. Union Panamericana.
  La vivienda en El Salvador. Washington: Union Panamericana, 1950.
  Comite Ad Hoc del Alianza para el Progreso.
    Evaluación del Plan Nacional de Desarrollo Economico y Social de El Salvador, 1965–1969. Washington: Union Panamericana, 1966.

Organization of American States.
  "Final Reports of the CIAP Subcommittee on El Salvador." Mimeographed. September, 1965; October, 1966; December, 1967; January, 1969. Washington: Pan American Union.
  Secretariat.
    "Domestic Efforts and the Needs for External Financing for the Development of El Salvador." Mimeographed. September, 1964; September, 1965; August, 1966; November, 1967; November, 1968. Washington: Pan American Union.

United States. Department of State. Agency for International Development [AID].

"Capital Assistance Paper: El Salvador, Construction of Rural Roads." Mimeographed. 1965.

"Capital Assistance Paper: El Salvador, National Housing Finance Agency." Mimeographed. 1967.

Country Assistance Program: El Salvador. 1963.

Country Assistance Program: El Salvador. Parts I and II. 1964.

Guatemala

LAWS

"Decreto Num. 132." November 1954.

"Decreto Ley 345." May 13, 1965.

Diario de Centroamerica. 1956–1967.

Diario Oficial. 1956–1967.

OFFICIAL GOVERNMENT PUBLICATIONS

Banco de Guatemala.
  Estudio económico y memoria de labores Año 1968. Guatemala, 1969.

Consejo Nacional de Planificación Económica.
  Informe de la República de Guatemala al CIES, 1961–1965. Guatemala, 1966.
  Informe de la República de Guatemala al CIES, 1966. Guatemala, 1967.
  Informe de la situación económica de Guatemala y sus perspectivas hasta 1972. Guatemala, 1968.
  La planificación en Guatemala: su historia, problemas y perspectivas. Guatemala, 1969.
  Primeros linamientos para el programa de inversiones públicas, 1965–1969. Guatemala, 1965.
  Programa de transportes de la República de Guatemala, 1965–1969. Guatemala, 1965.
  La situación del desarrollo económico y social de Guatemala. Guatemala, 1965.

Instituto Cooperativo Interamericano de la Vivienda.
  Carateristica del problema de vivienda en Guatemala, por Ing. L.F. Toledo Saenz. Guatemala, 1964.

Instituto Nacional de Administracion para el Desarrollo.
Informe del primer semenario nacional sobre administración para el desarrollo municipal. Guatemala, 1967.

Instituto Nacional de Vivienda [INVI].
Diagnostico preliminar del problema de la vivienda en Guatemala. Guatemala, 1967.
Informe presentado por el INVI ante la tercera reunion del subcomite de vivienda, edificación y planeamiento del Istmo Centroamericano. Guatemala, 1965.
"Informe trimestral, prestamo 39–TF/GU." Mimeographed. Guatemala, 1968.

Ministerio de Comunicaciones y Obras Públicas.
El programa del Instituto Cooperativo Interamericana de la Vivienda. Guatemala, 1960.
"Guatemalan Road Maintenance, May 1955 to May 1959; Final Report of Tippetts-Abbett-McCarthy-Stratton Inter-American Corporation." Mimeographed. Guatemala, 1959.
Direccion General de Caminos.
Memorias, 1957, 1958, 1959, 1960, 1961, 1962, 1963, 1964, 1965, 1966, 1967. Guatemala.

Ministerio de Hacienda y Credito Público.
Resúmen del presupuesto por programas para el año fiscal 1965. Guatemala, 1965.
Dirección Técnica del Presupuesto.
Control y medición de resultados del presupuesto por programas de los Años 1965, 1966, y 1967. Guatemala.

OTHER PUBLICATIONS

Organization of American States.
"Final Report of the CIAP Subcommittee on Guatemala." Mimeographed. December, 1966; February, 1968. Washington: Pan American Union.
Secretariat.
"Domestic Efforts and the Needs for External Financing for the Development of Guatemala." Mimeographed. January, 1966; October, 1966; February, 1968; February, 1969. Washington: Pan American Union.

Organización de Estados Americanos. Union Panamericana. Comité Ad Hoc del Alianza para el Progreso.
Evaluación del Plan Nacional de Desarrollo Económico y Social

de Guatemala, 1965–1969. Washington: Union Panamericana, 1966.

Secretaria Permanente del Tratado General de Integración Ecónomica Centroamericana.
    Guatemala: perspectivas de la inversión pública para el trienio 1968–1970. Guatemala, 1967.

United States. Department of State. Agency for International Development.
    "Guatemala: Highway Construction and Maintenance, Evaluation and Recommendations with Equipment List for the Improvement of Guatemala Highway Maintenance Operations." A Report Prepared by Paul Tysinger of the Bureau of Public Roads. Mimeographed. May 24, 1964.
    "Memorandum." Mimeographed. January 8, 1965. Guatemala.

World Bank. International Bank for Reconstruction and Development.
    The Economic Development of Guatemala. Washington, 1959.

Honduras

LAWS

"Decreto Num. 30." January 1, 1957.
"Ley Num. 30." October 1965   .
"Decreto Ley Num. 40." February 1955.

OFFICIAL GOVERNMENT PUBLICATIONS

Consejo Nacional de Economía.
    Diagnostico de vivienda. Tegucigalpa, Honduras, 1962.
    Informe nacional del progreso económica y social de Honduras. Tegucigalpa, Honduras, 1966.
    Plan bienal de construcciones de vivienda popular en Honduras, 1963–1964. Tegucigalpa, Honduras, 1962.
    Plan nacional de inversiones públicas del gobierno de Honduras para el periodo 1963–1964. Tegucigalpa, Honduras, 1963.
    Programa de inversiones públicas. tomo II del Plan Nacional de Dessarollo Economico y Social de Honduras, 1965–1969. Tegucigalpa, Honduras, 1965.

Consejo Superior de Planificación Económica.
    Informe económico y social del Gobierno de Honduras para la V

Reunion de Consejo Interamericano Económico y Social. Tegucigalpa, Honduras, 1967.

Inversiones realizadas durante 1965: información para la evaluación del programa de inversiones públicas. Tegucigalpa, Honduras, 1966.

Inversiones realizadas durante 1966. Tegucigalpa, Honduras, 1966.

Inversiones realizadas durante 1967. Tegucigalpa, Honduras, 1968.

Plan de acción 1968–1971. Tomo 1. Tegucigalpa, Honduras, 1968.

Instituto Nacional de Vivienda [INVA].

Documento preparado para el Consejo Superior de Planificación. Tegucigalpa, Honduras, 1967.

Instituto de la vivienda y su función social en Honduras, 1968. Tegucigalpa, Honduras, 1968.

El problema de la vivienda en Honduras: sintesis. Tegucigalpa, Honduras, 1964.

El problema de la vivienda en Honduras, por Ruben Mondragón. Tegucigalpa, Honduras, 1968.

Ministerio de Communicaciones y Obras Públicas.

Memoria de la Secretaria de Communicaciones y Obras Públicas, Octubre, 1960–Septembre, 1961. Tegucigalpa, Honduras, 1961.

Dirección General de Caminos.

"Programa para matenimiento y mejoramiento de caminos 1959–1962." Mimeographed. Presentado por Brown and Root, S.A. Tegucigalpa, Honduras, 1958.

Ministerio de Fomento.

"Progress Report on Honduran Highway Maintenance Project, January 1956 to April 1957." Mimeographed. Submitted by Upham, Porter, Urquhart Associates. Tegucigalpa, Honduras, 1957.

Direccion General de Caminos.

"Proposal for Highway Maintenance Program." Mimeographed. Submitted by Upham, Porter, Urquhart Associates. Tegucigalpa, Honduras, 1957.

OTHER PUBLICATIONS

Banco Centroamericano de Integración Ecónomica.

"Resolución de directorio No. DI 41/66." Mimeographed. Tegucigalpa, Honduras, 1966.

Instituto Centroamericano de Administracion Pública.

Informe sobre la organización y funcionamiento de la Dirección General de Caminos de Honduras. San José, Costa Rica, 1968.

Organization of American States.

"Final Reports of the CIAP Subcommittee on Honduras." Mimeographed. January, 1966; February, 1967; October, 1967; October, 1968. Washington: Pan American Union.

Pan American Union.

Housing in Honduras. Washington: Pan American Union, 1964.

Secretariat.

"Domestic Efforts and the Needs for External Financing for the Development of Honduras." Mimeographed. September, 1964; October, 1965; November, 1966; September, 1967; September, 1968. Washington: Pan American Union.

Organización de Estados Americanos. Union Panamericana. Comité Ad Hoc del Alianza para el Progreso.

Evaluación del Plan Nacional de Desarrollo Económico y Social de Honduras 1965–1969. Washington: Union Panamericana, 1966.

United States. Department of State. Agency for International Development.

"Capital Assistance Paper: Honduras—Cooperative Housing." Mimeographed. 1964.

"Capital Assistance Paper: Honduras—Farm-to-Market Access Roads." Mimeographed. 1965.

"Capital Assistance Paper: Honduras—Forest Fire Access Road." Mimeographed. 1964.

"Honduras: Farm-to-Market Roads: Monthly Monitoring Reports." Mimeographed. September, 1968.

"Program Memorandum for Honduras." Mimeographed. 1967.

World Bank. International Bank for Reconstruction and Development.

Appraisal of Honduras Highway Maintenance Project. Washington, 1955.

Nicaragua

LAWS

"Decreto Num. 6." February 1953.
"Decreto Ejecutivo Num. 52." January 31, 1962.

OFFICIAL GOVERNMENT PUBLICATIONS

Banco de la Vivienda Nicaraguense.
Estudio de las necesidades de vivienda en Nicaragua y posibles soluciones al problema. Managua, Nicaragua, 1966.
Informes del BNV al Presidente de la República: programa de vivienda popular para el periódo 1969–1972. Managua, Nicaragua, 1968.
Instituciones de ahorro y prestamo. Managua, Nicaragua, 1968.
Organización del Departamento INVI del Banco de la Vivienda de Nicaragua. Managua, Nicaragua, 1967.
    Departamento Fomento de Hipotecas Aseguerdas.
    Balance General. Managua, Nicaragua, 1968.

Instituto Nacional de Vivienda.
Información del sistema nacional de ahorro y préstamo. Managua, Nicaragua, 1968.
Inversiones en vivienda a la fecha. Managua, Nicaragua, 1968.

Ministerio de Fomento y Obras Públicas.
Informe general del Ministerio de Fomento y Obras Públicas, 1961–1962, and 1963–1964. Managua, Nicaragua.
Memoria del primer seminario nacional de carreteras. Managua, Nicaragua, 1966.
    Departamento de Carreteras.
    Diez años al servicio de la partria, 1955–1965. Managua, Nicaragua, 1966.
    Evaluación integral del plan camabocho. Managua, Nicaragua, 1968.
    Informe general, 1954–1955, 1955–1956, 1956–1957, 1957–1958, 1958–1959, 1959–1960. Managua, Nicaragua.
    Los proyectos viales en Nicaragua y el control de su financiamiento. Managua, Nicaragua, 1968.
    Solicitud de financiamiento al Banco Centroamericano de Integración Económica para la reconstruccion Portezuela-Las Mercedes. Managua, Nicaragua, 1965.
    Solicitud del Gobierno de Nicaragua al Banco Interamericano de Desarrollo para el financiamiento de la construcción de proyectos Viales. Managua, Nicaragua, 1965.
    Solicitud de prestamo al Banco Centroamericano para financiamiento de las carreteras Puente Real-La Frontera

con *Honduras y Octal-Las Manos.* Managua, Nicaragua, 1963.

Archivo.

Información sobre emprestitos a Junio 30 de 1968. Managua, Nicaragua, 1968.

Ministerio de Hacienda y Credito Público.

Presupuesto general de ingresos y egresos de la República por programas 1968. Managua, Nicaragua, 1968.

Oficina de Planificación.

Estadisticos del sector público 1960–1966. Managua, Nicaragua, 1968.

Estudio de los servicios de transporte en Nicaragua 1950–1962. Managua, Nicaragua, 1964.

Estudio del sector público de Nicaragua: 1950–1962. Managua, Nicaragua, 1962.

Evaluación de la ejecución del programa de inversiones públicas 1965–1969 en el año 1965. Managua, Nicaragua, 1966.

Evaluación de la ejecución del programa de inversiones públicas 1965–1969 en el año 1966. Managua, Nicaragua, 1967.

Informe de la oficina de Planificación sobre el desarrollo económico y social de Nicaragua. Managua, Nicaragua, 1967.

Inventario de proyectos de inversión pública en ejecución en el año 1965. Managua, Nicaragua, 1965.

Plan nacional de desarrollo ecónomico y social de Nicaragua 1965–1969, parte II (Managua, 1965), p. 13.

OTHER PUBLICATIONS

Escuela Superior de Administración Pública para América Central.

Diagnostico y macroanalysis administrativos del sector público de la República de Nicaragua. San José, Costa Rica, 1964.

Organization of American States.

"Final Reports of the CIAP Subcommittee on Nicaragua." Mimeographed. October, 1965; January, 1967. Washington: Pan American Union.

Secretariat.

"Domestic Efforts and the Needs for External Financing for the Development of Nicaragua." Mimeographed. September, 1964; September, 1965, October, 1966; January, 1968; February, 1969. Washington: Pan American Union.

Organización de Estados Americanos. Union Panamericana. Comité Ad Hoc del Alianza para el Progreso.
Evaluación del Plan Nacional de Desarrollo Económico y Social de Nicaragua 1965–1969. Washington: Union Panamericana, 1966.

United States.
    Department of State. Agency for International Development.
        "Capital Assistance Paper: Nicaragua, Housing and Savings and Loan System." Mimeographed. 1966.
        Operations Report 1967: Nicaragua. Washington, 1967.
    Department of Transportation. Bureau of Public Roads.
        "The Bureau of Public Roads in Nicaragua." Mimeographed. 1967.
        "Report of Highway Maintenance Activities in Nicaragua." Mimeographed. By R. C. McIntire. 1963.

World Bank. International Bank for Reconstruction and Development.
    The Economic Development of Nicaragua. Baltimore, Md.: Johns Hopkins University Press, 1953.

Index

DESIGNED
BY AUDREY SINNOTT
COMPOSED, PRINTED, AND BOUND
BY HERITAGE PRINTERS, INC., CHARLOTTE, NORTH CAROLINA
TEXT LINES ARE SET IN TIMES ROMAN, DISPLAY LINES IN OPTIMA

Library of Congress Cataloging in Publication Data
Wynia, Gary W/Politics and Planners
Bibliography
1. Central America—Economic policy
2. Bureaucracy. I. Title
HC141. W94/330.9'728'05/72–1382
ISBN 0–299–06210–4